PLAYS FOR YOUNG PEOPLE

Philip Osment

PLAYS FOR YOUNG PEOPLE

Who's Breaking?

Listen

Sleeping Dogs

Wise Guys

OBERON BOOKS
LONDON
WWW.OBERONBOOKS.COM

This collection first published in 2006 by Oberon Books Ltd
521 Caledonian Road, London N7 9RH
Tel: 020 7607 3637 / Fax: 020 7607 3629
e-mail: info@oberonbooks.com
www.oberonbooks.com

A catalogue record for this book is available from the British Library.

ISBN: 978-1-84002-272-8

Cover design by James Illman

Contents

Dedicated to

Lea Parkinson
(1966–2000)

Noël Greig
(1944-2009)

Introduction

The four plays in this volume were commissioned by two of the country's leading young people's theatre companies (*Who's Breaking?* and *Sleeping Dogs* by Red Ladder; *Listen* by Theatre Centre; and *Wise Guys* by both companies).

They were written to be performed in youth clubs (Red Ladder) and schools (Theatre Centre) by professional actors and were aimed at 14–18 year olds.

There are four artistic directors whose vision, support and encouragement were key to their commissioning and development. **Rachel Feldberg** (Artistic Director of Red Ladder until 1993); **Kully Thiarai** who took over from Rachel until 1998; **Libby Mason** (Artistic Director of Theatre Centre until 1992); and **Rosamunde Hutt** the current Artistic Director of Theatre Centre. These people have all made significant contributions to this particular area of work and gave many now-established playwrights their first commissions. However I might well have not been involved with the work of these companies if I hadn't had the example and support of the writer **Noël Greig**. It was through going to see his plays for Theatre Centre that I became acquainted with this work and it was he who recommended me to Rachel when she was looking for a writer.

The writer's brief for these companies was one which allowed the playwrights to explore issues about which they felt passionate which were relevant to young people, in the format of an hour-long play which, for Red Ladder performances, was always followed by a discussion in small groups led by the actors and the stage manager. (Theatre Centre performances sometimes included a discussion, depending on whether the school timetable allowed it.)

Who's Breaking? (1989) was my first commissioned play. My first play *This Island's Mine* had recently been performed by Gay Sweatshop and had been written on an Arts Council bursary. Rachel wanted a play for youth clubs that dealt with sexuality, masculinity and gender identity. She felt that these issues weren't being adequately dealt with in youth clubs: the girls were encouraged to talk about their feelings and relationships and the boys were taken outside to play football. I am generalising and over-simplifying maybe, but there was some truth in this perception.

Rachel brought me to Leeds and together we visited youth clubs and youth centres in the city and around Yorkshire where I talked to young men about relationships and gender identities.

I decided that the best way of tackling some of the issues that came up would be to explore a relationship between a young man very like some of the people that I met and a gay man – a relationship that began with hostility and mistrust and ended in some sort of friendship. How was I to bring two such characters together? I arrived at a story about a young man who discovers that he has come into contact with the HIV virus. *Who's Breaking?* has since been performed by many companies and has often been funded by Health Awareness Projects. It is perhaps ironic that what was in fact a plot device to bring my characters together has led people to see it as a play about AIDS. However it is hardly surprising since fear and ignorance about AIDS was rife and the disease is still infecting and curtailing lives both in this country and more drastically in Africa and India.

Rachel was also concerned that Red Ladder productions should push the boundaries theatrically and should reflect the company's equal opportunities policy. She had decided to employ a deaf actor for the production which meant that there would also be an actor/signer on stage with him. She told me not to think about this while I was writing although later in rehearsals I re-wrote the character of Rob for that production and made him deaf – the deaf actor also played Malc who was not a deaf character.

Listen sprang directly from the production of *Who's Breaking?* During rehearsals the company began to learn to sign and I got to know Mark Staines, the deaf actor in question.

I also noticed how silent the young audience became when they saw the father and son in *Who's Breaking?* locked in their inability to communicate. I felt that a play that looked at such a relationship in more detail would be of interest to them.

So when, in 1990, Libby asked me to write a play for Theatre Centre, I suggested one about a young deaf man (to be played by Mark) and his relationship with his hearing father. The boy's deafness and the father's inability to accept the disability of his son would serve to enhance the estrangement between the two.

The one big difference between Red Ladder's audience and Theatre Centre's is that in youth clubs the young people are not coerced and can choose to opt out of the performance at any point – a choice they do not have in schools. There is always a point about 45 minutes in where the audience gets restless. Some leave to have a cigarette or to talk to a friend outside although interestingly they keep one eye on the play and return to watch the end. **Sleeping Dogs** was my attempt to write a tragedy for the youth club audience to see if they would stay with it. I was interested in using heightened language and intense emotions and in seeing how those young people responded. It was 1992 when the break-up of the former Yugoslavia was causing ethnic strife on a scale not seen in Europe since 1945. There had been stories in the newspapers of families being torn apart and neighbours getting caught up in the brutality of the-so called 'ethnic cleansing'. One story that received a lot of attention, if I remember it correctly, was of a pair of 'star-crossed lovers', one Muslim, one Serb, who had tried to escape together from Sarajevo and had been shot dead on a bridge out of the city where their families had to leave them for many days as it was impossible to reach them.

When Red Ladder commissioned the play Kully had just taken over and it was she who helped me to develop the play together with Noël Greig, the company's dramaturg. Their experience and skill were invaluable.

Wise Guys could be called son of *Who's Breaking?* It marked an attempt to return to some of the same issues but within a harsher 90s environment. Rosamunde and I wanted to look at young men involved in crime and drugs and open a debate about this with young people in schools. I was also keen to present a piece that used some of the idioms of physical theatre. Again I was concerned that it should be a piece of theatre that would hold the attention of that audience so they could not but choose to watch it. We agreed that it should be directed by Tony McBride with whom I'd worked as an actor and who had played Steve in Rachel's production of *Who's Breaking?*, Barry in *Listen* and Sefat in *Sleeping Dogs*. He has a huge commitment to and understanding of that audience. Rosamunde understood the need for a long development process and when Kully brought Red Ladder on board as co-producer the two companies generously funded this process.

Tony and I spent a week in Cumbria observing a Youth At Risk residential course for young people who had self-selected and who were caught in destructive patterns of behaviour. There were anecdotes recounted by the young people and violent confrontations between the young people and the workshop leaders, which found their way into the play.

We spent time working in schools in Derby exploring themes and styles and talking to the pupils about their experiences. We were given the opportunity to explore every draft with actors and a choreographer, and there is no doubt that this process benefited the play and the production enormously. Tony worked closely with Lea Parkinson whose imaginative choreography brought a physicality to the play that made it very exciting to watch. Lea, to whom this volume of plays is dedicated, was one of those movement directors who enable actors to take risks because they feel totally safe and supported and it is a great sadness to the people who worked with him that his life was cut short.

I feel very privileged to have worked for Red Ladder and Theatre Centre not least because of the inspirational dedication and passion of the people involved in those companies as directors, administrators, education and outreach workers, actors, designers, composers and choreographers without whom these plays would not have been written. Most importantly these two companies provided and continue to provide a context for creating plays for an audience that needed to see them.

Philip Osment
February 2005

Since 2005 when this volume was first published, the importance of work for young audiences has been recognised by a wider range of venues and funders. There seems to be a greater willingness to prioritise young audiences and to produce work that speaks to their concerns. Venues such as Contact Theatre in Manchester, The Unicorn, The Roundhouse, Theatre Royal Stratford, The Lyric Theatre Hammersmith and Polka Theatre in London and newer venues such as Corby Cube cater specifically to those audiences and have engagement and outreach programmes accompanying the work. At the same time the Arts Council has promoted new companies such as 20 Stories High in Liverpool who are taking the work into new and interesting directions. Theatre for Young People is seen as being a career path for young theatremakers and there has been an increase in academic interest in the work reflected in Applied Theatre courses at both first degree and postgraduate level. This bodes well for the future of the work and gives it a vital role in the cultural life of the country.

Philip Osment
February 2012

WHO'S BREAKING?

Characters

STEVE
late teens

LINDA
late teens, Steve's girlfriend

MALC
late teens, Steve's best mate

CHRIS
early twenties, a volunteer at an AIDS Advice Centre

ROB
early twenties, Chris's boyfriend

Other characters and the CHORUS played by the cast.

Who's Breaking? was first performed in September 1989 by Red Ladder Theatre Company, with the following cast:

STEVE, Tony McBride

LINDA, Anna Ashby

MALC / ROB, Mark Staines

CHRIS, Andy Burke

Director, Rachel Feldberg

Signed by Jake Arnott

CHORUS:

The chorus is made up of the four actors. 1, 2 and 3 are men, 4 is a woman.

4: Saturdays.
1: Best day of the week.
2: Even if our team's just lost.
3: Making plans for a night on the town.
1: See you down the pub.
3: Game of pool before we go to the club.
4: Bonaparte's,
1: Fancy place,
2: Newly opened,
3: Loadsa birds.
4: Tweet, tweet, tweet.
2: Get home from the match.
3: If they're playing at home.
1: Mam, I'm back, where's me tea?
2: You'll get no bloody tea till you've cut that grass.
1: But Dad, I'm going out tonight.
2: You said you'd do it a week ago.
1: I'll do it tomorrow, promise you, Dad.
4: Leave him, Bill, his tea will get cold.
2: Too bloody soft on him that's your trouble.
1: Finish your tea, then it's upstairs for a bath.
3: Only to find the bloody door's locked.
1: Who's in there?
4: Me.
1: Well, hurry up.
2: I'll be late for me mates.
4: I'm washing me hair so you can bloody well wait.
1: Families,
2: It won't be like this when I've got one,
3: Oh, I want to get married,
4: Raise kids of my own,
1: I thought about six,
2: Three boys,
3: Three girls,

1: But not till I'm old,
4: About twenty-five.
1: But one thing's for sure,
2: My kids will all know,
3: That my word is law,
1: And what I say will go.
4: So you're in the pub by twenty to eight,
2: And you needn't have hurried 'cause the others are late,
3: A game of pool,
4: Another jar,
1: Discussing the match in the public bar,
2: Then it's off down the club for a few more pints,
3: (*Using a current club hit.*) 'They know'
1: 'What is what'
4: 'But they don't know'
3: 'What is what'
2: 'They just strut.'
3: Spotting the talent.
2: Perhaps trying to score.
1: Unless of course
   You're spoken for.

Scene 1

The club.

LINDA: Steve, Steve, over here.
STEVE: There you are. Malc, over here in the corner!
LINDA: Oh, you haven't brought him with you.
STEVE: (*To MALC.*) Get me another pint. You want one?
LINDA: Yeah.
STEVE: Linda'll have one. No, she'll have a pint. Tightfisted
    sod. (*Sings.*) 'I'm gonna get myself connected.' (*He starts to
    dance with her.*)
LINDA: Get off you daft bugger. Where've you been?
    Thought you weren't coming.
STEVE: Pub. (*He continues trying to make her dance. He bumps
    into someone.*) Sorry love. (*He rolls his eyes as if he finds the girl
    very attractive.*)

LINDA: (*Laughs.*) Been getting tanked up with your mate, have you?

STEVE: 'S right.

LINDA: Don't know why you always have to bring him.

STEVE: He's me mate.

LINDA: Your little lamb.

STEVE: He's harmless.

LINDA: Sometimes think he's jealous of me.

STEVE: Don't talk crap.

LINDA: Anyway you're lucky I'm still here. Bloke kept asking me to dance.

STEVE: Just landed, had he?

LINDA: Hey?

STEVE: What planet was he from?

LINDA: Very funny.

(*He kisses her.*

MALC comes up with the drinks.)

MALC: (*Pointedly.*) Don't mind me.

STEVE: (*Taking the drinks.*) Thanks mate.

MALC: Prices in here. Flash a few lights in your face and expect you to take out a mortgage to come here.

LINDA: Don't worry, Malc, I'll buy the next round.

MALC: Full of bloody queers, too. Whole group of 'em at the bar. Make sure you don't drink outa nobody else's glass. Never know what you might catch.

STEVE: You'll be alright, mate, just keep your back to the wall.

MALC: Alright, then, Lin?

LINDA: Yes thanks, Malc. You?

MALC: I'm alright.

STEVE: She reckons some bloke's been after her.

MALC: Hard up, was he?

LINDA: Oooh, you're such a comedian, Malc.

STEVE: Who was it anyway?

LINDA: Lenny Richards from work.

(*MALC and STEVE splutter into their drinks.*)

STEVE: My name's Lenny Richards and I work in personnel at Next.

MALC: Bloody ponce.

LINDA: There's nothing wrong with working at Next. 'Least we're not on the dole.

(*MALC and STEVE wince.*)

Anyway, I thought he was your mate.

STEVE: No. His brother was, Barry.

MALC: You heard about him?

STEVE: Who?

MALC: Barry Richards.

STEVE: What about him?

MALC: He's really ill they reckon.

LINDA: Yeah. Lenny said their Mam's got to go over to Manchester to look after him.

STEVE: What's wrong with him, then?

MALC: Dunno. Serious though. Oh no, look at that.

STEVE: What?

MALC: Them two blokes dancing together.

STEVE: Where?

MALC: There.

LINDA: Oh, yeah.

MALC: That's bloody disgusting that is.

STEVE: (*Laughing.*) What a sight.

MALC: Ugh, 'nough to turn your stomach.

LINDA: They're really good looking an' all.

STEVE: Get away, Lin.

LINDA: They are. It's a real shame.

MALC: How can you say that? Bloody perverts.

LINDA: If you dressed like that you might stand a better chance, Malc.

STEVE: Who with? The lasses or the lads?

MALC: Piss off.

(*STEVE makes up to MALC in quite a camp way.*)

STEVE: Oh, Malcy sweetie, didn't mean it. Give us a kiss.

(*He tries to dance with MALC.*)

MALC: You're bloody mad you.

STEVE: No I'm not. (*He starts singing again.*) 'I'm connected.' Come on, Lin, let's have a dance.

LINDA: Look after our drinks, Malc.

STEVE: If one of them comes up and asks you for a dance,
  just say you're spoken for.

CHORUS:

2: At half past twelve you're chucked out of the club.
3: Out of the warmth and the sweat and the noise,
4: It's cold outside and it's starting to drizzle,
1: And you stand there shivering in your t-shirt and jeans.
2: But you say to your mate,
3: By God, it's parky.
4: And you've had a few drinks.
1: So you don't give a damn.
3: Let's run for the bus.
1: No, I'm feeling peckish.
2: Well, what shall we have?
1: Pancake roll and chips.
4: So you walk down the street to the Chinese takeaway,
1: Trying to avoid the lads looking for a fight.
2: Whistling at lasses,
3: And chanting about United.
4: It's great being a lad on a Saturday night.
1: On the bus going home you have a row with the driver,
3: Sorry, lads, no chips on the bus.
1: So you stand to one side and eat them up quickly,
2: And jump on the bus just before he drives off.
4: Sitting upstairs with the windows all steamy,
1: Trying to make out if this is our stop.
3: Going round a corner you start to feel queasy,
1: Oh, I wish I hadn't had that sweet and sour bluuuurgh.
3: Oh, God, he's thrown up.
2: Shh, the driver will hear you.
  Let's get off before he comes up.
4: We can't get off here,
  We're only on the ring road.
1: I've got to get off before I do it again.
2: So you end up walking the last mile and a half,
3: Staggering along with frequent stops.
1: And you open the back door as quietly as possible,

2: But you still hear a voice saying,

4: Is that you home?

1: Which wakes up your Dad
   And he starts to grumble:

2: 'Bout bloody time too.
   I'll be waking you at nine to cut that grass.

1: You get yourself upstairs,

2: And fall into bed,

3: Reaching out to switch off your bedside light.

4: As you drift into sleep the last thought you remember is

1: What a way to spend your Saturday night.

Scene 2

Pub. A pool table. The actors don't play with real balls but mime their shots. LINDA and STEVE play some shots. LINDA takes aim. STEVE moves round the table and puts his finger where he thinks the ball should hit the cushion.

LINDA: Alright. I know.
   (*He keeps moving his finger.*)
   Cut it out, Steve.
   (*STEVE continues.*
   LINDA deliberately hits the ball so that it comes off the table and hits him in the groin.)

STEVE: Owww.

LINDA: Good shot, eh?

STEVE: (*Picking up the ball.*) Great. (*He continues playing.*)

LINDA: So when can we go flat hunting?

STEVE: Not Saturday.

LINDA: Why not?

STEVE: I'm going to the match with Malc.

LINDA: Steve.

STEVE: What?

LINDA: I thought you were fed up of living with your Mum and Dad.

STEVE: I am.

LINDA: You never seem very keen on looking.

STEVE: Well…

LINDA: What?

STEVE: I don't know if I can afford it.

LINDA: We could manage on my wages.

STEVE: Be your toy boy?

LINDA: Hardly.

STEVE: Thank you.

LINDA: Anyway you might get a job.

STEVE: Pigs might fly.

LINDA: Oh God, what's he doing here?

STEVE: Who?

LINDA: Malc.

STEVE: I told him we'd be in here.

LINDA: Is he coming to see the film with us an' all?

STEVE: Yeah, he can hold the popcorn. 'Lo Malc.

    (*MALC enters.*)

MALC: Hello, lovebirds. (*To LINDA.*) Hello, sexy.

    (*She doesn't respond.*)

    Oh, don't be like that.

LINDA: Like what, Malc?

MALC: You love it, sexy.

LINDA: Is that true, Malc?

STEVE: Cut it out, you two.

MALC: Yeah, you all like to think you turn us on.

LINDA: You should know, Malc. You're the expert.

MALC: Yeah.

STEVE: Fancy a game, Malc?

MALC: Alright.

LINDA: We haven't finished this one yet.

STEVE: Come on then.

MALC: Heard the latest on Barry Richards?

STEVE: No.

MALC: It's AIDS.

STEVE: Who told you that?

MALC: His sister told our Tracey.

STEVE: I don't believe it.

LINDA: It's true.

STEVE: How d'you know?

LINDA: Lenny told me.

MALC: They reckon he hasn't got long. Is he queer, then, Steve?

STEVE: Don't be bloody daft.

MALC: Thought you'd know seeing you was such good mates.

STEVE: Piss off.

LINDA: It's drugs.

MALC: You what?

LINDA: He caught it sharing needles.

STEVE: (*To LINDA.*) Your shot.

MALC: Barry Richards a junkie? He was into all that bodybuilding.

LINDA: Was he a junkie, Steve?

STEVE: No.

MALC: He might be queer though. They reckon a lot of those bodybuilders are. They might just be saying it's drugs.

STEVE: Look, are we playing this bloody game?

LINDA: Alright. Keep your hair on.

MALC: I reckon they ought to round up everyone with AIDS and put 'em all in quarantine, like, so they can't pass it on.

LINDA: You mean like dogs with rabies.

MALC: They shouldn't be given any food – they should just be allowed to die quickly.

STEVE: You talk such bloody rubbish sometimes, Malc. Do you ever listen to what comes out your mouth. You just open it and say the first thing in your head. And seeing as you're full of shit it's mainly crap that comes out.

MALC: Oooh, bloody hell. Someone's touchy tonight.

Scene 3

STEVE on the telephone. Surreptitiously.

STEVE: Hello?
  Oh, hello.

2: Remember Barry?

3: The health fanatic?

4: Down at the gym
  Working out?

2: Remember those mirrors?

4: Men preening and posing?

3: Watching your muscles
   Bulge and relax?

STEVE: Yeah. Uh… I wanted to know if I'm – if I might've
   caught it.
   Someone I used to know has got it – he's dying – and I'm
   worried like.

2: 'Just one more weight,' he said.

3: 'Just one more circuit.'

4: 'Breathe through the pain.'

2: 'It's doing you good.'

STEVE: We shared needles.
   No. Steroids. Down the gym.

2: 'Try some of this,' he said.

3: 'Gives you more stamina.'

2: 'Try some of this.'

4: 'Makes your body hard.'

STEVE: 'Bout two years ago.
   Not any more. Got bored with working out. Only injected
   it a few times. Gave me spots anyway. No. (*He looks at
   his arms as if looking for marks.*) Don't think so. (*He feels the
   glands in his throat.*)

2: 'Look at Barry,' they said.
   'His body's amazing!'

4: 'Look at his muscles.'

3: 'Wouldn't like to get on the wrong side of him.'

STEVE: I was wondering about going to the doctor –What's
   one of them?
   Oh, you mean the clap clinic.
   There's one up the hospital. They could give me a test
   there, couldn't they?

2: 'He's jobless and broke
   But you gotta respect Barry.'

3: 'Look at his body,
   It's a work of art.'
   (*STEVE looks around as if someone is coming.*)

STEVE: Look, I gotta go now.

No, it's OK. I'll be alright.

Yeah, I will.

(*FATHER enters.*)

Yeah. Thanks. Bye.

(*He puts the phone down.*)

FATHER: Alright, lad?

STEVE: Yeah.

FATHER: Who were you talking to?

(*STEVE doesn't respond.*)

I have to pay the bill.

STEVE: Mum pays the bill.

(*FATHER picks up the national newspaper.*

STEVE switches on the TV.)

FATHER: Turn that down.

(*STEVE scowls at him but does so using the remote control. He keeps changing channels.*)

Make your bloody mind up.

(*STEVE turns the TV off. Sits bored. Jiggles his leg.*)

Stop bloody fidgeting.

(*STEVE stops. Picks up the local newspaper.*)

There's some jobs in there you should look at.

(*STEVE puts the newspaper down. Starts jiggling his leg again.*

His father looks at him.

He stops. He looks at his hands, his nails. Starts to bite his nails.)

Don't bite your nails, lad.

(*STEVE continues to do so.*)

MOTHER: Yoo hoo, I'm back.

(*The other two don't respond.*)

Bloody buses. Had to wait half an hour outside work.

Then when it came it was only going half way,

Had to wait for another in the High Street.

Make us a cup of tea, Steve.

STEVE: I'm going out.

(*He goes.*)

MOTHER: What's wrong with him?

FATHER: How should I know?
    Time was,
    My lad would tell me everything.
    Time was,
    If he was troubled,
    I always knew.
    We formed a club for mutual admiration,
    With a membership that was limited to just us two.
    Kicking a ball around down on the playing fields,
    Or going out fishing down by the canal,
    I thought my son was all I'd ever wanted,
    I wasn't just his Dad,
    I was his best pal.
    Now we sit at home
    And no words pass between us.
    Except 'What's on telly?'
    And 'What have you done to your hair?'
    What we shared,
    Now causes us embarrassment,
    So we hide it,
    Bury it,
    Forget it was ever there.

Scene 4

STEVE in his bedroom getting ready to go out. He looks in the mirror. He changes his shirt. Before he puts his shirt on he feels under his arms. Looks at himself again. Puts on his shirt, buttons it. Starts to comb his hair.

FATHER: (*Off.*) Steve.
    (*STEVE stops combing his hair.*)
    You up there?
STEVE: Yeah.
FATHER: Linda's here.
STEVE: Send her up, then.
    (*He looks around his room, puts the shirt away.*
    LINDA enters.)
LINDA: 'Lo handsome.

STEVE: 'Lo.

LINDA: I brought the *Advertiser* round. There's a flat in it.

STEVE: Right.

LINDA: New shirt?

STEVE: Yeah.

LINDA: 'S nice. (*She goes to put her arms round him.*) Suits you.

STEVE: (*He avoids her.*) He'll be up knocking on the door in a minute.

LINDA: He's gone out in the garden. (*She puts her arms round him again.*)

STEVE: You're sex-mad, you are.

(*LINDA stops. Lets her arms drop. Sits down. Pause.*)

What's the flat?

LINDA: I've marked it.

(*STEVE opens the newspaper.*)

STEVE: Forty quid a week!

LINDA: There's nothing cheaper.

STEVE: Well, we can't afford it.

(*Pause.*)

Wanna go down the pub later?

LINDA: I got to go up the hospital with me Mam.

STEVE: Why?

LINDA: Me Uncle's poorly.

STEVE: Who? Your Uncle we went to Alton Towers with?

LINDA: Yeah.

STEVE: What's wrong with him?

LINDA: Well, nobody's supposed to know.

STEVE: Why not?

LINDA: 'Cause he's got cancer and they haven't told him yet.

STEVE: Why haven't they told him?

LINDA: Me Auntie doesn't want him to know.

STEVE: That's terrible that is, not telling the poor bloke.

LINDA: Some people would rather not know.

STEVE: Well I bloody well would.

LINDA: Well, so would I, but still –

STEVE: He's got a right to know.

LINDA: He's got a right not to know an' all.

STEVE: Crap.

LINDA: What's wrong with you tonight?

STEVE: Nothing.

LINDA: You're so bloody-minded you. Always know best.

STEVE: I don't.

LINDA: You bloody do. Always trying to tell people how to run their lives.

STEVE: When have I ever told you how to run your life?

LINDA: You moan about me working at Next. You don't like my friends.

STEVE: Like Lenny poncey Richards.

LINDA: That's what I mean. Just 'cause you don't like him you think nobody should. 'Least he doesn't try and push people around.

STEVE: Perhaps you should be going out with him then.

LINDA: Yeah, perhaps I should. He wouldn't make me feel like a nympho just for giving him a hug.

(*Pause.*)

STEVE: I didn't want me Dad walking in on us.

LINDA: I was only putting me arms round you. I didn't want to get into bed with you. Sometimes I think you don't even like me.

STEVE: 'Course I bloody do.

LINDA: Well you got a funny way of showing it.

STEVE: Come here.

(*She hesitates.*)

Come on.

(*He goes and puts his arms round her.*)

CHORUS: The STD Clinic.

2: Clench your fist
   Thank you.
   This won't hurt.
   And release it.
   OK.
   Just a bit more.
   Right.

Hold this cotton wool over the vein.

Good.

STEVE: I hate blood tests.

Make me faint.

2: Just sit there for a while and recover. The results should be through in about two weeks. So make an appointment to come back and see us then.

STEVE: That's it.

Outside again.

With just three days to worry.

Scene 5

The pub. STEVE and MALC are playing pool.

MALC: You alright, mate?

STEVE: Yeah, why?

MALC: You don't seem to have your mind on the game that's all.

STEVE: No, I'm alright. Your shot.

(*MALC plays.*

STEVE watches.)

Heard any more about Barry?

MALC: Barry who?

STEVE: Barry Richards.

MALC: Oh him, naw.

(*He watches the ball he has just hit.*)

Go on, go on – ohhhhh bugger.

(*He hands the cue to STEVE.*)

STEVE: How'm I supposed to get out of that?

MALC: Snookered. Must've been up to something though, mustn't he?

STEVE: Who, Barry?

MALC: Yeah.

STEVE: Suppose so.

MALC: Course he has. You don't get it from thin air.

STEVE: Thought you were scared of catching it from drinking out of a glass.

MALC: Don't die of ignorance.

STEVE: Shit.

(*He hands the cue back to MALC. Watches.*)

MALC: (*Looking at the table.*) Hmm.

STEVE: What would you do?

MALC: Mmm? (*He plays his shot.*) Oh, look at that. Steve
    Davis, eat your heart out.

STEVE: Not bad.

MALC: (*Sizing up the next shot.*) What do you mean what
    would I do?

STEVE: If you found out you had it.

MALC: (*Taking aim again.*) AIDS?

STEVE: Yeah.

MALC: Dunno.

(*He plays his shot.*)

(*Watching the ball.*) Shoot meself, I reckon. Missed the
bugger. Your go.

(*He hands the cue to STEVE.*)

CHORUS:

4: Come in and take a seat, Stephen.

2: Now as I explained last time there's no test for AIDS.

3: What we can tell you is whether you're body positive,

4: Which means that you've been in contact with the
    HIV virus –

2: That's the virus that causes AIDS –

3: And from your test this does seem to be the case.

STEVE: This social worker's got a crumb,

There,

On the side of her mouth.

Must've just had a biscuit,

I keep on expecting it to drop off.

But it stays there.

4: Now Stephen, this really isn't the end of the world,

2: Some people remain body positive for years before
    developing any symptoms.

3: The important thing is to keep healthy.

4: Do you smoke?

2: Alcohol?

31

4: Do you still go to the gym?

3: Sport?

2: Swimming?

4: And of course if you're having penetrative sex,
    Always use a condom.

3: Avoid taking risks of any kind.

STEVE: Perhaps I should tell her.
    It's annoying me, like.
    She could just lick it away with her tongue.
    Or flick it away with her hand.
    Perhaps I should reach out and brush it off for her.

4: Now it's important that you talk to someone about this,

2: So perhaps when you've had time to think you'd like to
    drop in at the Advice Centre.

4: They have regular meetings.

3: Thursdays,

2: Seven o'clock.

STEVE: I wonder what sort of biscuit it was?
    Plain digestive by the look of it.
    She must've had it in her tea break.
    Funny to think of her sitting here telling people
    What she's telling me.
    Then taking a tea break.
    Like any other job.

3: Here's the address and telephone number.

4: Now it's been quite a shock, Stephen.

2: But as I said it's not the end of the world.

3: I'm always here if you want to talk to me.

4: Are there any questions you'd like to ask? (*Pause.*)

STEVE: Can I go now?

2: Out in the Street in the hustle and bustle.

3: Walking along like he's in a dream.

4: Stopping off at the bus station kiosk.

3: Hello, lad.

STEVE: A Mars bar, a Twix, and a packet of fags.

2: On the top of the bus looking out of the window.

3: Seeing familiar sights go by.

4: Seeking some comfort in nicotine and chocolate,

STEVE: Trying not to hear the noise in his head.

4: Hello, love, been for an interview?

2: What's wrong wi' you?
  You look half dead.

4: Alright I was only asking.

2: Don't bloody talk to your mother like that.

3: Upstairs, alone in his bedroom.

2, 3 & 4: 'Stumble you might fall
  Stumble you might fall.'

4: Steve, your dinner's on the table
  Are you coming down for it?

STEVE: No thanks
  I don't want any thing to eat.

2, 3 & 4: 'Stumble you might fall.'

2: Malc's at the door
  Are you going to the pub wi' 'im?

STEVE: I'll see him later,
  I'm going to have a bath.

2, 3 & 4: 'You must be blind if you can't see
  The gaping hole called reality.'

4: Linda's on the phone.
  Steve, can you hear me?

STEVE: Tell her I'm busy.
  I'll ring her back.

Scene 6

The Advice Centre.

CHRIS: Hello.

STEVE: Hello.

CHRIS: You come for the body positive meeting?

STEVE: Err, yeah.

CHRIS: No one else is here yet. I don't think people start
  arriving till half past.

STEVE: Oh, I see.

CHRIS: My name's Chris. I'm learning how to be a volunteer.

STEVE: I'm Steve.

CHRIS: Steve. Right. Do you want a drink? There's no coffee because the urn hasn't boiled but they've got apple juice, pineapple juice, no orange, tropical fruit or Perrier – well, it's not Perrier, but it's the same thing only cheaper.

STEVE: Oh, yeah.

CHRIS: Which?

STEVE: Orange.

CHRIS: No, they haven't got any orange.

STEVE: Oh, err, apple.

CHRIS: Right.

(*He gets STEVE a plastic cup of juice.*)

Did you have far to come?

STEVE: Quite a way. I live over in Endsley.

CHRIS: Here. (*He hands him the drink.*)

STEVE: Ta.

CHRIS: That's not very far. Only takes five minutes in the car.

STEVE: I walked.

CHRIS: You live on your own?

STEVE: No, with me Mam and Dad.

CHRIS: Must be awkward.

(*Pause.*)

This your first time, then?

STEVE: I only had the result of me test the other week.

CHRIS: How you coping?

STEVE: Okay, like. It's difficult to grasp really.

CHRIS: Yeah.

STEVE: Don't think it's sunk in.

CHRIS: Must take time to adjust. Talking to other people who are going through the same thing will help.

STEVE: What happens at these meetings?

CHRIS: Well, last week was my first week. They spent the first half talking about business – you know, finances, fund-raising, arranging meetings with other groups in the area. Then they had a talk on alternative medicine.

STEVE: What's that?

CHRIS: The speaker was a homeopath.

STEVE: Lot of it about isn't there?

(*They both laugh.*)

CHRIS: Then they split up into small groups.

STEVE: What for?

CHRIS: To talk.

STEVE: What do they talk about?

CHRIS: Depends. Things like, you know, anger. Lot of people feel very angry.

STEVE: When I heard about the bloke I got it off I felt sorry for him. Then when I got me result I wanted to kill him.

CHRIS: Mmmmm.

STEVE: I only went round with him for about six months.

CHRIS: Do your Mam and Dad know about you and him?

STEVE: No, me Dad would kill me.

CHRIS: Yeah, well, when I told my parents, my Dad said to me I'd rather you were dead.

STEVE: When did you tell them?

CHRIS: Ages ago.

STEVE: How long have you known?

CHRIS: Since I was twelve.

STEVE: Hey?

CHRIS: I've got one mate who says he knew he was gay when he was six. It's not fair is it? It's hard enough growing up gay in a straight world without all those bastards saying what we do is evil and AIDS is the punishment for it. I'd be more than angry if I was body positive. I mean it makes you want to kill, doesn't it?

STEVE: Errr – yeah.

CHRIS: I mean that's why they have this gay men's group tonight. So we can all bitch about straights.
(*Pause.*)
I don't mean that. Some of my best friends are straight.
(*He laughs.*)
You got many straight friends?

STEVE: Yeah.

CHRIS: Last week someone said we shouldn't have anything to do with the straight people who use the centre. I don't agree with that, though. I know straight men can be really boring but they can't help it. Sometimes they even say something sensible. Do you want another apple juice?

STEVE: Uhhh, no… I err… I just remembered… I've got to go.

CHRIS: You what?

STEVE: I'm meeting somebody. I forgot.

CHRIS: Can't you rearrange it? You can use the phone if you want.

STEVE: No, it's alright.

CHRIS: You sure?

STEVE: Yeah.

CHRIS: Well, come back later. We'll be here till ten.

STEVE: Yeah, right, I will. Bye.

CHRIS: Bye.

(*STEVE goes.*

CHRIS stands looking puzzled. Slowly his mistake starts to dawn on him.)

(*Under his breath.*) Shit.

Scene 7

LINDA and STEVE in bed.

LINDA: Steve?

STEVE: Mmmmm?

LINDA: You're lying on my arm.

STEVE: Ohh. Sorry.

LINDA: You okay?

STEVE: Yeah.

LINDA: Doesn't matter, you know.

STEVE: What doesn't?

LINDA: We don't have to do it every time we go to bed.

(*Pause.*)

STEVE: When will your Mam and Dad be back?

LINDA: Not till late. They're over at me Auntie's. My Uncle's home for the weekend.

STEVE: Better then, is he?

LINDA: He'll have to go back in again for treatment.

STEVE: Does he know it's cancer yet?

LINDA: No.

(*Pause.*)

Saw a flat advertised in the newsagent's today. Thought we could go round and see it.

STEVE: Don't you ever talk about anything else?

LINDA: Heh?

STEVE: Flat this, flat that. Give it a rest.

LINDA: I thought you wanted us to live together.

STEVE: Not if you're going to bloody nag, I don't.

(*Pause.*)

Don't bloody sulk.

LINDA: I'm not.

STEVE: You keep going on about it. Pisses me off.

(*Pause.*)

LINDA: Owwww. Get off.

STEVE: Come on.

LINDA: You're hurting me.

STEVE: You like it.

LINDA: Leave me alone.

STEVE: Can't bloody win, can I? One minute you're complaining 'cause I don't give you enough attention. Next minute, you don't want me to touch you. Bloody women. Never know what they bloody want.

LINDA: And you never change your mind about anything, I suppose. Like you haven't changed your mind about the flat. It was your idea. Not mine. Only went along with it because you were so desperate to get out of home.

STEVE: Felt sorry for me did you?

LINDA: No.

STEVE: I don't need anyone feeling sorry for me.

LINDA: What's wrong wi' you, Steve?

STEVE: Nothing's wrong wi' me. Just shut up.

(*Pause.*)

I'd better be getting home.

LINDA: They won't be back for another hour.

STEVE: Still…

LINDA: Please yourself.

STEVE: I'll give you a ring.

LINDA: OK. What about the flat?

STEVE: Dunno.

LINDA: We'll leave it shall we?
STEVE: Yeah.
LINDA: I'll see you around then.
STEVE: Yeah. See you round.

CHORUS:

2: Down by the canal,
3: Place to go when you need to think.
4: Rat swims by,
2: Where?
4: There, by that red ball,
3: Half deflated,
4: Poking up through the oily film on the water.
2: Oh yes. I see him.
3: Further along two boys on the towpath fishing.
2: Hey Kev, give us some more bait.
4: Hang on, I think I caught one.
STEVE: Me Dad used to bring me down here. When I was
   a kid.
FATHER: They're all junkies and queers. They bring it on
   themselves.
3: There's a dog with the boys,
   Runs along the towpath,
   Comes to inspect the lad sitting there.
   Sniffs his shoes,
   Decides that he's friendly.
   Lies down beside him with his nose in his paws.
STEVE: We'd take them home to Mum and show her what
   we'd caught.
MOTHER: You make sure you're careful
   Don't want you getting that.
3: Dog catches sight of the rat in the water,
   Stands on the bank,
   Ears cocked,
   Head to one side.
   Wagging his tail,
   Growling and barking,
   Disturbing the quiet

And frightening the fish.

2: Here, Scamp,
  Cut that out.

STEVE: Then later, used to come down here night fishing,
  With Malc.

MALC: Shoot meself I reckon.

3: Now dog takes a plunge into the water,
  Nose in the air,
  Legs working away,
  He swims towards rat
  Who sees him coming,
  And makes a dash for his hole in the bank.
  So dog turns round and comes back to the towpath,
  Hauls himself out and shakes himself dry.
  Then proceeds on his way as if nothing has happened,
  The rat forgotten,
  His head held high.

LINDA: Steve didn't you ought to use a condom?

2: Come on, Scamp,
  We're going home now.

4: As they pass him by
  They show him their catch
  Proud of their day's work
  Carefree.

2: The two boys and their dog disappear along the canal,

4: And the rat pokes its nose out the hole once again.

STEVE: He's never felt so alone in his life.

Scene 8

The Advice Centre. STEVE enters.

CHRIS: Hello.

STEVE: How do.

CHRIS: There's no meeting tonight, I'm afraid.

STEVE: I wanna see a counsellor.

CHRIS: Right.

STEVE: A proper one.

CHRIS: I'll make you an appointment. Thursday okay?

STEVE: Can't I see anybody tonight?

CHRIS: She's not in tonight.

STEVE: Oh.

CHRIS: Shall I put you down?

STEVE: It's okay.

(*He starts to go.*)

CHRIS: Look –

STEVE: Yeah?

CHRIS: I'm sorry about the other night.

(*STEVE doesn't respond.*)

Got into trouble about it.

STEVE: Oh yeah?

CHRIS: They're only letting me do mail outs and answer the phone now.

STEVE: Come down here every night, do you?

CHRIS: Two nights a week. Just finished. Been licking envelopes.

STEVE: What you get out of it?

CHRIS: I'm unemployed at the moment. Go mad sitting at home.

STEVE: Yeah. Know what you mean.

CHRIS: So I thought I'd help out.

STEVE: But you're not HIV.

CHRIS: I know people who are.

STEVE: Gays.

CHRIS: Yeah.

STEVE: So you do it because you're gay?

CHRIS: Well…

STEVE: Anyone can get AIDS you know.

CHRIS: I'm sorry. It was the gay men's meeting. I just assumed…

STEVE: Yeah, well you shouldn't assume, should you?

CHRIS: No. I shouldn't.

STEVE: 'Cause I'm not.

CHRIS: I know.

STEVE: I'm just a boring straight.

(*The phone rings.*)

CHRIS: Hang on.

(*He picks it up.*)

Hello, AIDS advice. (*To STEVE.*) Don't go.

Oh, hi, Rob. I'm just leaving. I'm going to get us a takeaway.

But you said you were staying at my place tonight.

Well, how late will you be?

I see. Where are you going?

Thought we were going to see that together on Friday.

You going on your own?

Who you going with then?

Didn't know he was in town.

I'm not.

I'm not.

Alright I'll see you later.

(*He puts the phone down.*)

What were you saying?

STEVE: Saying how straight and boring I was.

CHRIS: So what did happen?

STEVE: What?

CHRIS: How did you…?

STEVE: Sharing needles.

CHRIS: I see.

STEVE: No you bloody don't. Think I'm a junkie now, don't you? We were doing stuff down the gym: anabolic steroids – ever heard of them? So I'm not gay and I'm not an addict. I'm really straight. I'm surprised you got the time to talk to me, really. You should run home to your mate and bitch about me.

CHRIS: Look, why did you run off the other night?

STEVE: Well…

CHRIS: Yes?

STEVE: You thought I was gay.

CHRIS: So? Is that so terrible?

STEVE: And you said all those things.

CHRIS: About straights?

STEVE: Yeah.

CHRIS: Well, sometimes if does feel as if they're to blame. The government only started to do something about AIDS when they realised straights could get it as well.

STEVE: So you only want to help out the gays. That makes you just as bad.

CHRIS: That's not what I said.

STEVE: Bet you were glad to see the back of me the other night.

CHRIS: When you realised I was gay you couldn't get out of here quick enough. You nearly gagged on your apple juice you drank it so fast. So yes, I thought: if it worries him that much then I hope the little shit doesn't come back.

(*Pause.*)

That what you want to hear?

STEVE: They'll keep you on licking envelopes if you talk to people like that.

(*CHRIS laughs.*)

CHRIS: So why did you come back?

STEVE: I wanted to talk to the counsellor.

CHRIS: Even if she's queer?

STEVE: What?

CHRIS: Nothing.

STEVE: Is she?

CHRIS: My big mouth. Was there no one you could talk to?

STEVE: No.

CHRIS: Mates?

STEVE: They'd think I was –

CHRIS: Gay?

STEVE: Yeah.

CHRIS: Girlfriend?

STEVE: What about her?

CHRIS: Does she know?

STEVE: No.

(*Pause.*)

We don't always use condoms.

CHRIS: I see. You could talk to her about safe sex.

STEVE: I couldn't.

42

CHRIS: Why not?

STEVE: She'd wonder what was going on. Anyway you don't talk about them things to your girlfriend.

CHRIS: I do to my boyfriend.

> (*The phone rings.*
> *CHRIS picks it up.*)
>
> Hello?
>
> Hi.
>
> No, I'm still talking to someone.
>
> Mind your own business. No-one you know.
>
> Yes, I bloody am pissed off.
>
> I'll phone you tomorrow.
>
> Because I can't talk now.
>
> I'll talk to you tomorrow.
>
> Yeah. Bye.

STEVE: That your err…

CHRIS: Me boyfriend. Yeah. (*Looking at his watch.*) Nine o'clock.

STEVE: (*Starting to leave.*) Yeah, I'll see you.

CHRIS: Fancy a drink?

STEVE: Eh?

CHRIS: I suddenly seem to have a free evening.

STEVE: Well…errr…

CHRIS: You're not scared about someone seeing you walking through town with me, are you?

STEVE: No.

CHRIS: Sure? I wouldn't want to embarrass you.

STEVE: Yeah, I'm sure.

CHRIS: Right, so shall we go then?

STEVE: Okay.

Scene 9

MALC playing pool on his own. LINDA enters and watches. MALC looks up and sees her.

MALC: Hello.

LINDA: 'Lo Malc.

MALC: Meeting Steve?

LINDA: Why?

MALC: Just wondered.

LINDA: Is he coming down here tonight, then?

MALC: Dunno. Thought he might be.
   (*Pause.*)

LINDA: When did you see him last?

MALC: Can't remember. Last week I think.

LINDA: Oh.

MALC: You two go down Bonaparte's Saturday, did you?

LINDA: No. Went with me friend.

MALC: What was Steve doing, then?

LINDA: I thought he must've been out pubbing with you.

MALC: No. (*Pause.*) Two-timing you, is he?

LINDA: What you mean?

MALC: I'm ready and waiting for you, Linda.

LINDA: You know something I don't?

MALC: Joke. He's been keeping funny company lately
   though.

LINDA: Hey?

MALC: Saw him from the bus the other night. Walking along
   the High Street with this bloke.

LINDA: So?

MALC: I recognised him.

LINDA: Who was it?

MALC: Remember when we saw them poofs down
   Bonaparte's.

LINDA: Yeah.

MALC: Well, this bloke Steve was with was one of them.

LINDA: You're having me on.

MALC: 'S true.

LINDA: How would Steve know a bloke like that?

MALC: I don't know. Here, perhaps he's on the turn.

LINDA: You are having me on. You're bloody mad, you are.

MALC: You can ask him yourself. He's just come in. (*Calling
   out.*) Steve. Over here.
   (*STEVE enters.*)

STEVE: 'Lo Malc. Linda.

LINDA: 'Lo.

STEVE: Alright?

LINDA: Yeah. You?

STEVE: Yes, thanks.

MALC: Want a drink, mate?

STEVE: No, thanks. I only popped in for some fags.

MALC: Where you off to then?

STEVE: I'm going to see a film.

LINDA: Who with?

STEVE: Oh, uhhh…my cousin.

LINDA: What cousin?

STEVE: Eh?

LINDA: What cousin?

STEVE: You haven't met him.

LINDA: Or is it a she?

STEVE: What?

LINDA: Nothing.

MALC: You want one, Lin?

LINDA: No thanks. I got to go too. I'm being took out for
a meal.

MALC: Oh yeah. Where to?

LINDA: Benbow's Bistro.

MALC: Flash. Wondered why you were tarted up.

LINDA: Yeah, well. Some people know how to make a lass
feel wanted.

MALC: I'll get me own then.

(*He hands STEVE his cue and goes to the bar.*)

LINDA: What's her name, Steve?

STEVE: What you talking about?

LINDA: The lass.

STEVE: What lass?

LINDA: The one you're seeing tonight.

STEVE: I'm not seeing any lass. Who you going to Benbow's
Bistro with, anyway?

LINDA: Lenny.

(*STEVE starts playing pool.*)

Steve?

STEVE: (*He tries to play a shot.*) Excuse me.

LINDA: Sorry.

STEVE: Don't let me keep you.

LINDA: No. Alright. Bye then.

STEVE: Bye.

(She goes.

STEVE looks at his watch.

MALC returns.)

MALC: Gone then, has she?

STEVE: Yeah.

MALC: Bloody slag.

STEVE: Shut your mouth, you.

MALC: She is. Reckon she only came in here so she could boast about going down Benbow's Bistro with Lenny Richards.

STEVE: I told you to shut it.

MALC: She's two-timing you mate. Bloody slag.

STEVE: *(Grabbing MALC.)* I told you to shut your mouth.

MALC: Keep your hair on. You've spilt me drink.

STEVE: *(Giving him a coin.)* Here, buy yourself another.

(He goes.

MALC watches him.)

CHORUS:

2: A candle-lit dinner
   In Benbow's Bistro,

3: There's couples at tables
   Eating avocado prawns.

2: Talking in whispers

3: Smiling politely

4: Using their napkins
   To stifle their yawns.

2: D'ye like your steak rare?

3: *Pommes frites* or croquette?

2: Have some mayonnaise.

3: I prefer vinaigrette.

4: Over there is a couple,

2: They come here each week.

3: They've got nothing to say

4: So they eat but don't speak.

2: Lenny leans over
    And pours out more wine.
3: You're very quiet.
4: I'm feeling fine.
3: Chocolate gateau?
2: Or fruit salad and cream?
4: My Dad says he's dependable,
    My Mum thinks he's a dream.
    And I sit there remembering
    All the mad times with Steve:
1: Walking along the towpath
4: Chips from the bag.
1: Driving home from Alton Towers
4: Hot dogs from a van.
    Or buying a late night burger,
    In the bus station café.
    And never
    Never yawning
    Never running out of things to say.

Scene 10

The gym. A social area near the exercise machines. Maybe there is a mat for stretching.

CHRIS: Steve, hi.
STEVE: Hello.
CHRIS: You made it then.
STEVE: Yeah. They've got a few more machines down here than they used to have.
CHRIS: Yeah.
STEVE: More weights an' all.
CHRIS: Aren't you going to go round?
STEVE: Didn't bring me gear. I know the instructor so he just let me in.
CHRIS: We did our induction with him.
STEVE: Have to take it easy to start with.
CHRIS: Don't half get some posers down here. Look at him.
STEVE: I used to see him down here when I used to come.

CHRIS: He's grotesque. (*Calls.*) Rob!

(*He points at the man they have been talking about, mimes a muscle-bound man and curls his lip.*)

How many of those have you done? Show off! Your back's not straight.

(*They watch ROB exercise.*)

STEVE: He's swinging his legs as well.

CHRIS: Stop looking at yourself in the mirror and come over here!

STEVE: It's better if you just lift your legs slowly with that one.

(*ROB enters.*)

CHRIS: Rob, this is Steve.

ROB: How do.

STEVE: Hello.

CHRIS: We won't be much longer, Steve.

ROB: What time does the film start?

STEVE: Half eight.

ROB: We got plenty of time then.

CHRIS: Right I'm going to have a go on that one now it's free. I'll show you how you're supposed to do it, Rob. Watch.

ROB: Okay.

(*CHRIS goes.*)

Makes you sweat, doesn't it?

(*He drinks some water from a bottle and pours some over his head.*

Awkward pause.)

Did you come here from work?

STEVE: No. I'm on the dole.

ROB: Like Chris. (*He sees someone attractive.*) Wow, look at him. What a body.

(*They watch.*)

STEVE: Where do you work?

ROB: Addison's Dairy. I'm a gay milkman so I have to sleep with all the husbands.

(*STEVE doesn't know how to respond.*)

STEVE: Long way out there.

ROB: I go on my bike.

STEVE: Mountain or racer?

ROB: BMW. 750.

STEVE: (*Impressed.*) You're a biker?

ROB: You got one?

STEVE: I'd like one.

ROB: I'll give you a go on it sometime.

STEVE: Oh…err…right…thanks.

(*CHRIS returns.*)

CHRIS: See.

ROB: What?

CHRIS: Weren't you watching?

ROB: Forgot.

CHRIS: You left sweat all over that machine as well.

ROB: Can't help it. Here.

(*He throws his towel at CHRIS who ducks and it hits STEVE.*)

Sorry, Steve. Right I'm going to do my second set of twenty. (*He goes.*)

CHRIS: How are you?

STEVE: Funny being down here.

CHRIS: We could have met somewhere else.

STEVE: No, I wanted to come. Scene of the crime.

(*Pause.*)

CHRIS: How are things with Linda?

STEVE: Not too good. I think we might be splitting up.

CHRIS: Oh dear.

(*CHRIS looks at ROB.*)

STEVE: Who's that he's talking to?

CHRIS: Dunno. Yeah, alright. We're watching. Yeah that's better. But don't swing your legs.

STEVE: You and him live together do you?

CHRIS: No, we decided not to.

STEVE: How come?

CHRIS: I don't know. We wanted to keep our independence.

STEVE: Oh, you don't want to get tied down like. I can understand that. It's like me and Linda.

CHRIS: What is?

49

STEVE: Well, she wanted us to settle down together and I wanted me freedom.

CHRIS: I didn't mean that.

STEVE: What did you mean, then?

CHRIS: Me and Rob are committed to each other. But we don't want to be like a married couple. We want to give each other space.

STEVE: Makes you sound like astronauts. What does it mean?

CHRIS: Well, if one of us wants to be on his own in the evening, or to go off with friends then we come to some sort of arrangement.

STEVE: What if one of you wants to do something together and the other wants to do something on his own?

CHRIS: We talk about it.

(*ROB returns.*)

ROB: I'm shattered.

CHRIS: You haven't done your sit-ups yet.

ROB: You're a fanatic. You'll end up looking like Mr Muscle over there.

CHRIS: Who was the bloke in the blue vest?

ROB: You spotted him too did you? Met him at the match the other week. He's straight, unfortunately. No offence, Steve.

STEVE: You two United supporters?

CHRIS: I'm not. He is.

ROB: He doesn't like football.

STEVE: Why not?

CHRIS: I get scared when I see gangs of blokes on the rampage.

ROB: Going to Liverpool?

STEVE: Maybe.

ROB: How you getting there?

STEVE: Dunno.

ROB: Want a lift?

CHRIS: Rob.

ROB: Yeah?

CHRIS: You talking about this Saturday?

ROB: Yeah, it's the quarter final.

CHRIS: That's the day Dave's moving out.

ROB: Dave who?

CHRIS: Dave who lives upstairs from me. He's hiring a van. Said we'd go down to London with him and help him move into his new house.

ROB: First I've heard of it.

CHRIS: I told you the other night.

ROB: I don't remember.

CHRIS: You said you wanted to go to Old Compton Street afterwards.

ROB: Oh yeah.

CHRIS: So?

ROB: It's the quarter final. Anyway I've offered Steve a lift to Liverpool now.

CHRIS: You always do this.

ROB: You and Dave can go.

CHRIS: I'm fed up with it.

ROB: Don't start.

STEVE: Ummm…

CHRIS: What?

(*They both look at him.*)

STEVE: I can go on the train.

(*Pause.*

CHRIS does some stretches.)

ROB: Right. Now for that dumbbell.

(*He pretends to be an Olympic weightlifter, snatching breaths and looking as if he's in pain.*)

CHRIS: I'm going to go and get changed. See you in the café.

ROB: Okay.

(*ROB goes.*)

STEVE: I can go on the train you know.

CHRIS: No, it's alright.

STEVE: Giving him space, are you?

CHRIS: Something like that. See you outside.

CHORUS:

1: Saturday night.
2: Down the Chichester Arms.
3: Public bar's full of lads.

1: Getting tanked up.
2: The saloon bar, well, I won't say what's in there –
3: But it's something very queer.
1: What's happening next door?
2: Gay night.
1: Gay night?
2: Yeah, can't you tell?
4: Look just like any other crowd to me.
1: Blokes with pierced eyebrows and very tight t-shirts,
2: Girls with tattoos and studs in their tongues,
3: Club kids
4: And Goths,
1: Mohicans
2: And Skallies
3: There's even someone wearing a United scarf.
1: Which one?
3: The biker.
4: Time, gentlemen, please.
1: Drink up.
2: I'm coming.
3: What's the hurry?
4: Outside they're leaving in twos and threes,
1: Except for that one there on his own.
2: The biker wearing the United scarf.
1: He's going down by the canal,
    Come on, lads, let's get the bugger.
2: Hey, poof!
1: Did you hear?
    My mate's talking to you.
3: Oooh, the little lady's playing hard to get.
1: Sorry about that,
    Did I just give you a shove?
2: You wanna be careful you might fall in the canal.
3: He's getting away,
1: Grab him,
2: Trip him up.
3: Oooops, sorry about that.
1: Kick his head in.

2: That'll teach you.

3: Fucking queer.

2: There's someone coming.

3: Run.

2: Come on.

1: Alright.

4: One last boot,
   Then it's off along the canal,

2: Over the wall,

3: Through the gardens,

1: Up the ginnel.

2: And away into the night.

4: Leaving someone lying with blood streaming from his head.

2: A muddy scarf in the puddle beside him.

4: In a while a siren screams in the night.

Scene 11

The hospital.

STEVE: I came as soon as I got your message. How is he?

CHRIS: They don't know yet.

STEVE: How'd it happen?

CHRIS: After he dropped you off from the match he
   went down the Chichester Arms to the gay night. He
   took the short cut along the towpath and they must've
   followed him.

STEVE: Brought you this. (*He holds up a bottle of whisky.*)
   Thought you might need it.

CHRIS: Thanks. I just got back from London. He got
   someone to ring me.

STEVE: Have you been in to see him yet?

CHRIS: Just for a few minutes. He looked awful. I had to have
   an argument with the doctor.
   (*LINDA enters and STEVE catches sight of her.*)
   Didn't want to let me in because I'm not related to him.
   I said, 'Listen, sunshine, as far as you're concerned I'm his
   next of kin.'
   (*STEVE is trying to hide behind CHRIS.*)

53

What's up?

STEVE: Nothing.

LINDA: Steve? Thought it was you.

STEVE: What you doing here?

LINDA: Me Uncle's just been brought in again. Had a relapse.

STEVE: Bad?

LINDA: They're going to have to operate.

STEVE: They told him?

LINDA: They have now. How about you?

STEVE: Oh, err – someone's been beaten up.

LINDA: Get into a fight, did he?

CHRIS: It was a queerbashing.

STEVE: Linda, this is Chris.

LINDA: Hello, Chris.

CHRIS: How d'you do? I've heard a lot about you.

LINDA: Have you? You're his cousin then?

CHRIS: Pardon?

STEVE: No.

LINDA: So what happened to this mate of yours?

CHRIS: He was beaten up leaving the Chichester Arms.

LINDA: Been to the gay disco, had he?

CHRIS: Yes.

LINDA: Do you know who did it?

CHRIS: No.

LINDA: Probably some of your mates, Steve. (*Pause.*) Well, I
got to go or I'll miss me bus. See you, Steve.

STEVE: See you.

LINDA: (*To CHRIS.*) Hope your mate's alright.

CHRIS: Thanks.

(*She goes.*)

STEVE: That was Linda.

CHRIS: She seemed nice.

STEVE: Yeah.

CHRIS: What did she mean?

STEVE: About what?

CHRIS: About your mates.

STEVE: She was just stirring.

CHRIS: I don't understand.

STEVE: You know what lads are. The way they go out
   looking for fights.
CHRIS: Yes I do. So does Rob.
STEVE: That's all she meant.
CHRIS: You mean you've got mates who go queerbashing?
STEVE: They don't now.
CHRIS: But they used to.
STEVE: Yes.
CHRIS: Did you go with them?
STEVE: Mmmmm?
CHRIS: I said, did you used to go with them?
STEVE: I was there one night.
CHRIS: You mean you stood by and watched the others kick
   his head in.
STEVE: Chris –
CHRIS: Is that what you did? Or did you actually put the boot
   in yourself just to prove what a hardcase you were?
STEVE: It was ages ago. We didn't know any better.
CHRIS: Piss off, Steve.
STEVE: Look –
CHRIS: Here, take your bloody whisky and piss off. I don't
   want you here. I'm fed up listening to your problems. Go
   and find your mates and talk to them.
   (*STEVE hesitates.*)
   What you waiting for?
   (*STEVE goes.*)
   And don't bloody come back either.

Scene 12

*The bus stop. LINDA stands with an umbrella. STEVE is further off
looking at her.*

LINDA: A bus stop
   In the rain.
   And now we've run out of things to say.
   Hello, lover boy. Where's your boyfriend? Lost him
   have you?
STEVE: I want to talk to you.

LINDA: Sitting there like they were old friends.
　　Talking like they were old friends.
　　Talking. Like we haven't talked for weeks.
　　The horror on his face when he saw me.
　　Like I was something the cat had brought in.

STEVE: I want to explain.

LINDA: You don't have to explain to me, duckie. I've got
　　eyes. I'm not stupid.

STEVE: No?

LINDA: He'll see how I've missed him
　　If I show him my face.
　　And in his eyes I'll read what?
　　Pity? Distaste?
　　Malc told me he'd seen you out with a gay bloke but I
　　didn't believe him.

STEVE: For crying out loud –

LINDA: Come on, bus
　　Come and take me away –
　　I just hope you haven't caught anything –
　　Impossible to leave.
　　Agony to stay.

STEVE: What d'you mean?

LINDA: Well, there's no knowing what you might have
　　caught, is there?

STEVE: No, there's no knowing. (*He goes.*)

LINDA: This bus stop stands at the top of the hill
　　No shelter from the stormy weather.
　　So if I shiver
　　Remember
　　It's just the effect of the cold North wind.

CHORUS:

2: Three am.

3: In the city.

4: Walking through the underpass.

1: Car pulls up,

2: Two coppers looking,

3: What are you doing out this late, lad?

1: Later on, down by the station,
2: Standing on the railway bridge.
3: Watching goods trains passing under,
2: Feeling hopeless
3: Trying to find a way out:
STEVE: Looking down at the tracks
 And thinking how easy it would be.
 To stand up on the parapet,
 Wait till the train's nearly underneath,
 And just jump.
 No more worries,
 No more cares.
 Nothing.
 One coming now,
 Big heavy one,
 Diesel engine,
 Smoke billowing,
 Trucks rattling behind.
 See the lights on the front getting closer,
 Pulling you in,
 Only take a second.
 Going underneath now –
2 Da dum, da dum.
4: Da dum, da dum.
STEVE: That one's gone but there's another coming soon.

Scene 13

The railway bridge. STEVE is standing on the parapet.

CHRIS: Steve! Steve! Is that you?
 (*He approaches.*)
 Steve?
STEVE: Yeah?
CHRIS: I've been looking all over town for you. Where've
 you been all night?
STEVE: Walking round.
CHRIS: You're soaked through.
STEVE: 'S been raining.

CHRIS: Finished off the whisky, have you?

STEVE: Yeah. How is he?

CHRIS: They kept him in overnight. But he's going to be alright. He was lucky.

(*Pause.*)

Steve, I'm sorry.

STEVE: What for?

CHRIS: For getting angry. I was upset about Rob.

STEVE: Naw, you were right. I'm just a bad lot.

CHRIS: That's not true.

STEVE: Yes, it bloody is. Be better off dead.

CHRIS: Don't be daft.

(*Pause.*

STEVE walks along the parapet.)

Careful.

STEVE: You ever want kids?

CHRIS: Dunno. I don't think about it. I like children. Me sister's kids come and stay sometimes.

STEVE: I always said I'd have six. Huh. Won't even be getting married now.

CHRIS: You don't know that.

STEVE: Who'd have me? Linda? She'll run a mile when she finds out. And if she's positive too, she's really going to thank me.

CHRIS: She might want to help you through it.

STEVE: She won't.

CHRIS: How do you know? You haven't given her the chance. It's the worst feeling in the world hiding from people, pretending, lying. Believe me, I know, I spent my adolescence doing that. It was only when I came out that –

STEVE: For Christ's sake, don't you ever stop talking about being gay? It's not the same. You're not going to die of AIDS. I am.

CHRIS: You're living with AIDS not dying.

STEVE: It's just a matter of time. All the things you thought you were going to do with your life. Suddenly they're just wiped out. All you are is someone with HIV. Nothing else matters. It's like having a death sentence hanging over you. I'm so bloody scared, Chris.

(*He starts to weep.*

CHRIS watches him.)

CHRIS: 'Ere.

(*He gives him a handkerchief.*)

STEVE: Ta.

CHRIS: You should have done this a long time ago.

STEVE: Done what? Thrown meself over the railway bridge.

CHRIS: No. Admitted you were scared.

STEVE: I couldn't. I was too scared.

CHRIS: I know.

(*Pause.*)

What would they have felt if you had committed suicide? Your Mam and Dad and Linda? You've got to give them a chance. Give yourself a chance. The thing is to make the most of the time we've got however short or long it is.

STEVE: Birds are starting to sing. What do they call it?

CHRIS: The dawn chorus.

STEVE: That's it.

(*Pause.*)

Know one thing. If anyone had told me a couple of months ago that I'd be standing on this bridge at four o'clock in the morning talking about all this with a bloke like you then I'd've thought they were off their head.

CHRIS: Yeah, well, I never knew I could be friends with someone like you either.

Feeling better?

STEVE: Yeah.

CHRIS: Shall I give you a lift home?

STEVE: Ta.

CHRIS: Come on, then.

(*CHRIS holds out his hand.*

STEVE takes it. Then pulls CHRIS towards him and hugs him. Pause.)

Let's get you home.

STEVE: Right.

Scene 14

The pub. Pool table. MALC is playing on his own. STEVE joins him with two pints.

STEVE: Here you are, Malc.

MALC: Ta. Your go.

> (*STEVE starts playing.*)
> Did you get over to Liverpool for the quarter final the other week?

STEVE: Yeah, I got a lift.

MALC: We got right pissed that night when we got back.

STEVE: Where did you go?

MALC: Chichester Arms. I was well out of it. You should've been there.

STEVE: Mmmm.

MALC: You coming down Bonaparte's wi' me later?

STEVE: No, I'm meeting some mates.

MALC: I thought I was your mate.

STEVE: Eh?

MALC: I said I thought I was your mate.

STEVE: Your go.

MALC: Ta.

STEVE: Bloke got beaten up down the Chichester that night, I heard. That true? Got set upon by a group of United supporters.

MALC: You know how the lads can be.

STEVE: Know anything about it, Malc?

MALC: I heard he was queer.

STEVE: Makes it alright, does it?

MALC: What's got into you?

STEVE: Make you feel good, did it?

MALC: Look it weren't me. It was Tod and his lot.

STEVE: You know it was going on?

MALC: Might have.

STEVE: He was a mate of mine.

MALC: Who?

STEVE: The bloke who was beaten up.

MALC: The queer?

STEVE: Yeah, the queer.
  (*He takes the cue from MALC.*)
MALC: You on the turn then, mate?
STEVE: You asking me if I'm gay, Malc?
MALC: Yeah, sure.
STEVE: What if I were?
MALC: Oh, come off it, Steve.
STEVE: You never know.
MALC: You're having me on.
STEVE: You'll have to figure that out for yourself, won't you?
  (*He pots the final ball.*) Two games to me. Want another?
MALC: Uhh, no, I'll be off.
STEVE: OK, Malc. See you round. I'll be in here Tuesday.
MALC: Right.
STEVE: Bye then.
MALC: Yeah, see you Tuesday.
  (*MALC goes.*
  STEVE continues playing on his own.
  LINDA enters. Stands watching him.
  STEVE doesn't see her.)
LINDA: Steve?
STEVE: (*He turns.*) Well?
LINDA: Negative.
STEVE: Thank Christ.
LINDA: I gotta go back in three months for another. But we
  haven't been exactly close lately, have we? So they think
  that'll be negative too.
STEVE: Right.
LINDA: How've you been?
STEVE: Okay. Spending quite a bit of time down the Advice
  Centre. There's a group I go to.
LINDA: Yeah. Chris said.
STEVE: You went in and saw him did you?
LINDA: Yeah.
STEVE: Good. (*Pause.*) Well, thanks for coming and
  telling me.
LINDA: That's okay.
  (*Pause.*)

STEVE: I'll be seeing you then.

LINDA: Yeah.

> (*He goes back to the pool game.*
> *LINDA hesitates.*
> *His attention stays on the pool table.*
> *Suddenly she grabs the cue from him.*)

Why did it take you so long?

STEVE: Hey?

LINDA: Why didn't you tell me?

STEVE: I didn't know what you'd do.

LINDA: You should have told me. I didn't know what was going on. You had no right not to tell me. What did you think I was going to do?

STEVE: Dunno. Go off with someone I suppose.

LINDA: Don't blame Lenny Richards. The way you were behaving. Not telling me what was going on. Going all quiet and moody.

> (*Pause.*)

Look at you. You're doing it now.

STEVE: I'm not.

LINDA: You bloody are.

> (*Pause.*)

STEVE: I was scared of losing you, Lin.

> (*Pause.*)

LINDA: You playing?

STEVE: Okay.

LINDA: You break.

> (*They start to play.*)

STEVE: What you doing tomorrow?

LINDA: Me Uncle's taking me hang-gliding.

STEVE: Your Uncle who's got cancer?

LINDA: 'S right.

STEVE: Bloody hell, what happens if he pegs out up there?

LINDA: Wouldn't be a bad way to go.

STEVE: They'd never get him down again, he'd just float off.

LINDA: He said he's always wanted to do it. So he's blown all his savings on a glider.

STEVE: I wouldn't mind doing that.

LINDA: You asking me if you can come?

STEVE: Yeah.

(*CHRIS enters.*)

CHRIS: Sorry I'm late.

STEVE: That's okay.

CHRIS: Rob's just parking up the bike. Oh, hello, Linda.

LINDA: Hello.

CHRIS: I didn't know you were going to be here.

LINDA: No, well, perhaps I should be off.

CHRIS: No, stay. Was it alright?

LINDA: Yeah.

CHRIS: Good.

(*The three of them look at each other.*)

STEVE: You've moved on from licking envelopes then.

CHRIS: Yeah. Oh, look, I spoke to the landlord about the flat
    above mine. He said if you're interested you should give
    him a ring.

STEVE: Oh, oh right. Good.

CHRIS: Who wants a drink?

STEVE: Half, please.

CHRIS: Linda?

LINDA: Please.

(*CHRIS goes.*)

STEVE: I was going to tell you.

LINDA: Sounds familiar.

STEVE: I didn't think you'd want to…

LINDA: What?

STEVE: Move in with me.

(*ROB enters.*)

ROB: Right you lot. Let me show you how to play this game.

STEVE: This is Rob, Lin. Rob, this is Linda.

ROB: Hi Linda.

LINDA: Hello.

ROB: You've got very good taste in boyfriends.

LINDA: Have I?

ROB: Don't you think so?

LINDA: Maybe.

ROB: Well, if you ever get bored with him just pass him onto me.

(*CHRIS returns with the drinks.*)

LINDA: Wanna do a swap do you?

(*They both look at CHRIS.*)

CHRIS: What?

ROB: Nothing.

(*ROB and LINDA laugh.*)

STEVE: (*Holding the cue.*) Shall we have a foursome?

(*The other three look at him in alarm.*)

I meant at pool.

CHRIS / ROB / LINDA: Ohhh.

ROB: Alright. Me and Steve against Linda and Chris.

CHRIS: You're on.

STEVE: Heads or tails?

(*He throws a coin in the air.*
They all look up.)

CHORUS: (*Hang-gliding.*)

1: Up with the birds,

2: Flying high.

3: Looking down at the earth,

4: From a clear blue sky.

LISTEN

Note on reading the play

The play is written to be performed with a deaf actor playing Ian using his own voice. What is being said should be clear to hearing audiences from the way characters respond to each other. An interpreter is necessary for deaf audiences.

When Ian is with his mother he uses his voice and some signs. With his father he relies more on his voice and mime. He lip-reads them both very well. His mother uses some simple signs to communicate with Ian but this might change when they are with his father because he disapproves of sign language. Lucy is partially hearing and lip-reads and speaks quite clearly. With Ian she signs although for Jeff's benefit she might sometimes use her voice. There are times when she signs because she doesn't want Jeff to understand what she is saying.

All underlined lines are signed and not spoken.

BSL/Sign Supported English

With his mother Ian uses Sign Supported English but he and Lucy communicate in BSL. I have tried to use simple language that is easily translatable but obviously the words and their order often change in BSL and lines such as 'Jeff has got some money' becomes 'Jeff money have.' It is therefore important that someone who understands the idioms of both BSL and spoken English works with the actors on these translations.

Characters

SHARON
early forties

BARRY
her husband, mid-forties

IAN
their son, sixteen

LUCY
Ian's friend, late teens

JEFF
Lucy's boyfriend, late teens

The play was originally performed with the actors playing Sharon and Barry doubling as Lucy and Jeff. Alternatively it can be performed with a cast of five.

If possible the Judge Dredd characters should be made visual with the actors playing Sharon and Barry putting on masks and taking up the comic strip poses. But this does mean that costume changes have to be very slick!

Listen was first performed in September 1990 by Theatre Centre, with the following cast:

SHARON / LUCY, Ali Belbin

BARRY / JEFF, Billy Braham

IAN, Mark Staines

Director, Libby Mason

Designer, Kate Owen

Sign Advisor, Iona Fletcher

Company Stage Manager, Debs Hart

Workshop Co-ordinators, Fiona Graham & Bridget Escolme

Education Officer, Becky Chapman

The second production had the following cast:

SHARON / LUCY, Yolande Bastide

BARRY / JEFF, Tony McBride

IAN, Mark Staines

Director, Philip Osment

Designer, Charlotte Malik & Kevin McKeon

Sound Tape, Debs Hart & Helen Pringle

Company Stage Manager, Helen Pringle

Workshop Co-ordinator, Graeme Urlwin

Pack compiled by Becky Chapman & Graeme Urlwin

Sign Advisor, John Wilson

Scene 1

The hospital.

SHARON and BARRY enter and sit side by side. Soundtrack of hospital. BARRY is itching. SHARON looks concerned. BARRY picks up a magazine. SHARON is watching people in the waiting room. A voice calls out a name. SHARON and BARRY look up, watch someone go through to the doctor. BARRY returns to his magazine. SHARON gets a packet of mints from her bag. Offers one to BARRY.

SHARON: Want one?

BARRY: No thanks.

> (*She takes one herself. Puts the sweets back in her bag. Sucks it noisily.*
> *BARRY looks at her.*
> *She stops.*
> *He returns to his magazine.*
> *SHARON looks at her watch.*)

SHARON: Always keep you waiting.

BARRY: They're overworked.

SHARON: Hmmm.

> (*She takes a book from her bag. Starts reading.*
> *Pause.*)

VOICE: Mr Brennan.

> (*SHARON and BARRY look up.*)

> Mr Barry Brennan.

BARRY: Yes.

VOICE: Doctor will see you now. Straight along the corridor.

> (*He hesitates.*)

SHARON: Shall I come?

BARRY: If you want.

> (*They go.*)

Scene 2

On the bus.

IAN is sitting looking out of the window. Soundtrack of bus. He takes
2000AD *from his bag. Starts to read it. The voices from the comic and*
the INSPECTOR are also on the soundtrack.

NARRATOR: 'A great darkness fell on MegaCity One.
  Sickness and death stalked its streets. There was talk
  of a new dark judge who had opened his soul to the
  corruption.'
INSPECTOR: Tickets please.
  (IAN continues reading.)
NARRATOR: 'They said his thirst for death was
  unquenchable and that as he slayed he wept.'
INSPECTOR: Ticket, mate.
  (IAN jumps as if he has just been tapped on the shoulder.)
  Can I see your ticket, please?
  (IAN takes travel pass and shows it to the INSPECTOR.)
  Thank you. Tickets please.
  (IAN goes back to his comic.)
NARRATOR: 'Beneath, hidden from view, the evil judges
  continue their ghastly work…guarding their secrets until
  the moment should come to reveal their creation…their
  masterpiece…their necropolis.'
  (IAN looks out of the window. Realises he has come to his stop.
  Gets off the bus. Sound of the conductor ringing the bell.)

Scene 3

Living/dining room.

SHARON enters. She has just come back from the hospital. Pause.
BARRY enters. Puts bottle of pills and car keys on the table. Pause.

BARRY: There's something wrong with that car.
SHARON: Yeah?
BARRY: Won't go in gear right.

SHARON: Have to get it seen to.

BARRY: Hope the clutch isn't going.

   (*Pause.*)

SHARON: Cup of tea?

BARRY: We just had two at the hospital. Might be low on
   fluid. I'll have a look later.

   (*SHARON goes and puts her hand on his shoulder.*)

   I'm not going to die tomorrow, you know.

   (*She takes her hand away.*)

   Nothing but trouble that car. Austin Aggro they call it.

   Can't afford a new one now though.

SHARON: I could get a job.

BARRY: We'll manage.

SHARON: What shall we have for dinner?

BARRY: Dunno.

SHARON: I got pork chops in the freezer.

BARRY: (*Doubtfully.*) Mmmmm.

SHARON: Well, what would you like?

BARRY: Don't mind.

SHARON: I could do frozen peas with them.

BARRY: Yeah.

SHARON: Ian likes chop.

BARRY: Let's have chops then.

   (*Pause.*)

SHARON: Or we could have egg and chips.

BARRY: (*Snapping at her.*) I don't care what we have.

   (*Pause.*)

   Ian will have to help.

SHARON: I know.

BARRY: What do you mean, you know?

SHARON: If you're going to be in and out of hospital –

BARRY: I didn't mean that. I meant with the car.

SHARON: Oh.

BARRY: If it is just the clutch fluid.

SHARON: You going to tell him?

BARRY: Tell him what?

SHARON: What the doctor said.

   (*BARRY doesn't respond.*)

You want me to talk to him?

BARRY: No.

(*Pause.*)

SHARON: He'll be home in a minute.

BARRY: What do you want me to say to him, eh?

SHARON: Don't know.

BARRY: You'd better start saving up for a wreath, son, because your Dad's about to kick the bucket?

SHARON: That's not what the doctor said.

BARRY: 'S what he implied.

SHARON: He said the success rate was getting better all the time.

BARRY: Has to say that, doesn't he?

(*IAN enters the house.*
BARRY and SHARON have not seen him.)

What's the point of telling him? It's not going to make me feel better if everybody knows, is it?

SHARON: I don't know.

BARRY: 'Course it ain't.

SHARON: I'll go and peel the potatoes. Or would you rather have baked?

BARRY: I don't care!

(*She goes.*
IAN enters.)

Hello son.

(*IAN doesn't respond. Sits down. Gets out the comic. Reads.*
BARRY taps the comic.)

Good day at school?

(*IAN grimaces as if to say so-so. Then continues reading.*)

Anything on the telly tonight?

(*IAN doesn't respond.*
BARRY taps the table.)

Ian.

(*IAN looks up.*)

What's on the telly tonight?

(*IAN shrugs as if to say he doesn't know.*
BARRY picks up the newspaper.
SHARON enters.)

SHARON: 'Lo, love.

   (*She kisses IAN.*

   He moves his head as if he didn't want her to.

   She stands behind him and addresses BARRY.)

   You told him?

BARRY: Told him what?

   (*He looks to see if IAN is watching.*

   IAN looks up.)

SHARON: That he's got to help you with the car.

BARRY: Oh that. (*He goes back to his paper.*)

   (*IAN is angry that they're talking about him. And signs at them angrily.*)

IAN: What are you talking about? You were talking about me. (*To his Mother.*) You were standing behind me. He was looking at you. What were you saying about me?

SHARON: (*Signing as well as speaking.*) I wasn't saying anything about you.

IAN: You were. Liar.

BARRY: Don't talk to your Mother like that.

   (*IAN signs something rude.*)

SHARON: Ian!

BARRY: Use your voice. What did he say?

SHARON: Your Dad wants you to help him with the car. I was just asking him if he'd told you.

IAN: Was that all?

SHARON: That's all.

   (*IAN shrugs as if he doesn't quite believe it.*)

   So go and change and you can do it before tea.

IAN: Homework.

SHARON: Do your homework after tea.

IAN: I'm going out tonight.

SHARON: Where you going? Lucy's?

IAN: Yes.

SHARON: Well, your Dad needs your help.

IAN: Tomorrow.

SHARON: That alright, Barry?

BARRY: What?

SHARON: He said he'll do it tomorrow.

BARRY: Mmm.

SHARON: That okay?

BARRY: Have to be, won't it?

    (*IAN gets up. Pulls a face at BARRY. Goes.*)

SHARON: Better finish these potatoes.

    (*She goes.*

    Pause.

    BARRY picks up IAN's comic. Looks at it.)

VOICE: 'You can't go back to MegaCity, Judge Dredd. Judges don't go back.'

DREDD: 'These aren't normal times. Trouble. Evil judges have taken over. We gotta fight these devils. Let's get going. Get that old jalopy started.'

    (*Noise of machines at amusement arcade.*)

Scene 4

Amusement arcade.

IAN and LUCY are having a signed conversation. Everything underlined is signed and not voiced.

IAN: <u>You got 50p?</u>

LUCY: <u>What for?</u>

IAN: <u>I want to play this machine.</u>

LUCY: <u>I'm broke. Jeff has got some money.</u>

IAN: <u>Where is he?</u>

LUCY: <u>He should be here.</u>

    (*They look at the machine.*

    JEFF enters. He calls LUCY from the door.)

JEFF: Lucy! Luce!

    (*He goes to LUCY and touches her.*)

LUCY: Hello. You got 50p?

JEFF: What for?

LUCY: Machine.

    (*JEFF gives her the money.*

    She gives it to IAN who puts it in the machine.)

    Watch out, you're going to crash.

JEFF: Slow down.

LUCY: Awwwwh.

   (*IAN giggles.*)

JEFF: Jammy.

LUCY: Overtake.

JEFF: Mind the bend.

LUCY: You're coming off the road.

JEFF: No he's not.

ALL THREE: Awwwh.

LUCY: Not bad. 1500. My go.

   (*LUCY takes the steering wheel.*)

IAN: (*To JEFF.*) I'm a good driver.

JEFF: Wait till you get in a real car.

IAN: I can drive.

JEFF: You're not even seventeen.

   (*IAN shrugs.*)

   Who taught you?

IAN: My Dad.

JEFF: Your Dad?

IAN: Yeah.

JEFF: Where did he teach you?

IAN: Bisley.

JEFF: Bisley? What, the old aerodrome?

IAN: Yeah.

LUCY: Oh, look at that. Wicked.

   (*IAN and JEFF watch her for a moment.*)

JEFF: What sort of car's he got?

IAN: Who?

JEFF: Your Dad.

IAN: XR3i.

JEFF: (*Impressed.*) XR3i, wow.

IAN: Yes. He's a test driver.

JEFF: He's a what?

IAN: A test driver.

JEFF: A test driver? Your Dad? Don't believe you.

IAN: It's true.

LUCY: Damn. (*She signs.*) <u>Shit.</u>

   (*IAN goes to look at her score.*)

JEFF: Here, Lucy, did you know that?

IAN: <u>1400.</u>

LUCY: What?

JEFF: His Dad's got an XR3i.

IAN: Your turn.

LUCY: <u>You been telling lies again?</u>

IAN: <u>No.</u>

JEFF: And he's a test driver.

LUCY: Who?

JEFF: His Dad.

LUCY: <u>What's all this about?</u>

IAN : <u>What?</u>

LUCY: <u>Why are you making up stories?</u>

IAN: <u>I'm not.</u>

LUCY: <u>Your Dad's got an old banger.</u>

JEFF: Here, here. What you two talking about?

LUCY: <u>And he's a lorry driver.</u>

IAN: <u>He's a test driver weekends.</u>

LUCY: Bullshit.

JEFF: Bullshit, I got that. Is he having me on?

IAN: No. (*He looks at LUCY.*)

JEFF: Is he, Luce?

LUCY: It's your go.

> (*JEFF holds the steering wheel.*)
> (*Behind JEFF's back.*) <u>Liar.</u>

IAN: <u>It's true.</u>

LUCY: <u>Piss off.</u>

IAN: <u>Piss off yourself.</u>

LUCY: <u>Stories, stories, stories.</u>

> (*JEFF turns to watch them.*
> *IAN and LUCY look at the screen.*)

IAN / LUCY: Look out.

JEFF: Awwwh. You two were distracting me.

IAN: (*Laughs.*) Three hundred. (*He giggles again.*)

LUCY: Sorry.

IAN: I win.

JEFF: Yeah, you win. You haven't passed your test yet though, have you? (*To LUCY.*) Me Dad's lending me the car bank holiday Monday.

LUCY: We could go somewhere.

JEFF: Yeah, that was the idea.

LUCY: Where shall we go?

JEFF: Dunno.

LUCY: Margate. We could go to Dreamland.

JEFF: OK.

LUCY: You wanna come, Ian?

IAN: Yes.

LUCY: (*To JEFF.*) It's alright if Ian comes isn't it?

JEFF: (*Halfheartedly.*) Sure.

IAN: I'll have to ask my Mum.

LUCY: Your Mum won't stop you, will she?

IAN: No.

LUCY: It'll be great.

    (*IAN looks at JEFF.*)

JEFF: Yeah.

LUCY: Let's have a go on this one.

JEFF: I said we'd see Andy and Trevor and Sue down the caff.

LUCY: Don't like that Sue. (*To IAN.*) Want a hamburger?

JEFF: She's alright.

IAN: Haven't got any money.

LUCY: Jeff will pay.

JEFF: What you saying?

LUCY: You'll pay for him, won't you?

JEFF: Yeah.

LUCY: Come on then.

    (*They go. More arcade noise on soundtrack.*)

Scene 5

The car.

BARRY and IAN are outside working on the car. SHARON is folding laundry in the house.

BARRY: (*At the engine.*) When I tell you, put the clutch in.
    Understand?

IAN: Yes.

BARRY: Right.

(*IAN puts the clutch in.*)

No not yet. Ian.

(*IAN looks up.*)

Not yet.

IAN: Sorry.

BARRY: I'll go like that. (*He puts his thumb up.*)

IAN: OK.

BARRY: Can't get this nut undone. Owhh. (*He stands up and shakes his hand.*)

IAN: (*Putting his thumb up.*) Yes?

BARRY: (*Angrily.*) No. Hurt my thumb.

(*IAN laughs.*)

It's not funny.

(*He bends over the bonnet again.*)

Ah, that's it. Now I'll just put in some fluid.

(*He does so. He has a can to catch the fluid that will come out of the pipe.*)

Alright, Ian.

(*IAN is not watching. He is playing with something on the dashboard.*)

Ian! Ian!

(*IAN looks up.*)

Watch!

IAN: Sorry. (*He puts the clutch in.*)

BARRY: No not yet.

(*IAN lets the clutch up again.*)

I have to catch the fluid that comes out. Never mind. (*He bends over the engine again.*) Right, let the clutch up.

IAN: What?

BARRY: Let the clutch up. (*He mimes this with his hand.*)

IAN: Up.

BARRY: For crying out loud! Keep it in till I tell you to let it up. Stupid.

IAN: I didn't know.

BARRY: Just do what I tell you.

(*IAN pokes his tongue out at him but BARRY doesn't see.*)

Right, we'll start again.

(*He bends over the bonnet.*)

IAN puts the clutch in.
The fluid squirts out.)
Hey. What you doing?

IAN: You said, 'Let the clutch up.' I had to push it in first.

BARRY: What?

IAN: (*Signing.*) You said, 'Let the clutch up.' The clutch was
    up. I pushed it in so I could let it up.

BARRY: Don't use all that deaf and dumb stuff with me. You
    know I don't understand it. Now come on. And don't be so
    thick. Wait for me to tell you.
    (*IAN gets out of the car.*)
    What you doing? Get back in that car.

IAN: No.

BARRY: Ian.

IAN: Get stuffed.

BARRY: Don't you be so cheeky. Get back in.
    (*He grabs hold of IAN.*)
    Do as I tell you.
    (*SHARON enters.*)

SHARON: What's going on?

BARRY: He's messing around.

IAN: He thinks I'm stupid.

SHARON: 'Course he doesn't think you're stupid.

BARRY: I do.

SHARON: Barry.

BARRY: Don't you take his side. He wants to learn a bit of
    respect.
    (*IAN pretends to be 'retarded'.*)
    And you can cut that out. You hear me?

IAN: No I'm deaf and dumb.

BARRY: And don't get funny with me lad.

IAN: I can't hear you. I'm a dummy.

BARRY: I've had just about enough of you and your cheek.
    Just cut it out.

IAN: Can't hear.

BARRY: I'll make you hear then. Teach you to get funny
    with me.
    (*BARRY lashes out.*

IAN cowers.)
SHARON: Don't, Barry.
BARRY: He's enough to try the patience of a saint.
(*He goes.*)
IAN: <u>Bastard.</u>
SHARON: Stop that.
IAN: He's a bully.
SHARON: He's got a lot on his mind.
IAN: I hate him.
SHARON: Course you don't hate him.
IAN: I do. I wish he was dead.
SHARON: What did you say?
IAN: (*Signs without speech.*) <u>I wish he was dead.</u>
(*SHARON slaps him.*
They look at each other for a moment.
SHARON goes.)

Scene 6

The bathroom and bedroom.

BARRY has washed his hands and face and is drying himself with a towel. He stands for a moment looking at himself in the mirror. Picks up a bottle of pills and a glass of water and takes two tablets. He goes to the window and closes the curtains. SHARON enters. BARRY lies on the bed.

SHARON: You alright?
BARRY: Bit tired, that's all.
SHARON: You're not supposed to get worked up.
(*BARRY says nothing.*
SHARON goes and sits on the bed.)
He doesn't understand, Barry.
BARRY: Understand what?
SHARON: Well, why you're…what's wrong with you.
BARRY: What do you mean, what's wrong with me?
SHARON: Why you got cross with him.
BARRY: I got cross with him because he was being a pain.
That's why I got cross with him.

(*Pause.*)

God, this itching.

SHARON: You'll be better after the treatment.

BARRY: Feeling all hot and sweaty too.

SHARON: Doctor said you would. (*Pause.*) Tina just phoned.

BARRY: Want you to go clubbing with her again, did she?

SHARON: She said she might be able to get me some work.

BARRY: Where?

SHARON: Down the betting shop. She's manageress now.

BARRY: You couldn't do that.

SHARON: I got a good head for figures.

BARRY: I'm not having you working at a bookie's. (*Pause.*)

SHARON: What time you got to be at the hospital tomorrow?

BARRY: Half eight. Have to finish bleeding the clutch.

SHARON: Yeah.

BARRY: Fluid was leaking.

SHARON: Mmnmm.

BARRY: Think I fixed it though.

SHARON: Good.

(*Pause.*)

BARRY: Gonna try and have a nap.

SHARON: Right. Shall I bring you up a cup of tea later?

BARRY: If you like.

SHARON: Okay.

(*She stands looking at him.*

He turns over and closes his eyes.

She goes.

BARRY stays lying there during the next scene.)

Scene 7

The living room.

IAN is watching TV. It is turned up really loud. Cops and robbers/car chase. SHARON enters and gets out the ironing. She looks at IAN. He ignores her.

SHARON: Ian. (*She touches him.*) Ian.

IAN: What?

SHARON: Turn the TV down.

IAN: Why?

SHARON: It's very loud.

(*IAN frowns. He turns the sound down.*)

Ian.

(*He looks at her.*)

I'm sorry.

(*He looks away.*)

Ian.

IAN: What?

SHARON: I want to talk to you.

IAN: Can I go to Margate with Lucy and Jeff?

SHARON: To Margate?

IAN: Yes.

SHARON: When?

IAN: Next week.

SHARON: I suppose so.

IAN: Great.

(*IAN looks back at the television.*)

SHARON: Ian.

IAN: What?

SHARON: Take your Dad a cup of tea and say sorry.

IAN: Say sorry to him? Why?

SHARON: Because.

IAN: What?

SHARON: There's a reason why he's touchy at the moment.

IAN: He's always touchy.

SHARON: No he's not. You've got to try and understand.

IAN: Why? He doesn't try and understand me. He thinks
I'm thick.

SHARON: He doesn't think you're thick.

IAN: He does. You always take his side.

SHARON: Oh, don't be daft. I'm not a referee. I told you,
he's got a lot on his mind.

IAN What?

SHARON: He's got to go back to the hospital tomorrow.

IAN: What for?

SHARON: For treatment.

IAN: I thought he was better.

SHARON: Well, he isn't better.

IAN: What's wrong with him?

SHARON: They think it might be serious.

IAN: Serious? Why?

SHARON: He's got cancer.

> (*Pause.*)
>
> They're pretty sure. But they don't know how far it's spread.
>
> (*She continues ironing.*)
>
> He saw the specialist yesterday and they told him.
>
> (*IAN just stares, nothing registers on his face.*)
>
> I went up to the hospital with him. The doctor said 'I'm not going to mince my words.' I thought that meant your Dad was going to have to go in for an operation or something. (*She continues ironing.*) He didn't say cancer at first. Non-Hodgkins lymphoma he called it. (*She stops to spell it out and puts the iron down.*) Non-Hodgkins lymphoma. I didn't know what it was. Then he started talking about radiotherapy and chemotherapy. Your father said, 'That's how they treat cancer.' And the doctor said: 'Non-Hodgkins lymphoma is a form of cancer.'
>
> (*Pause.*
>
> *IAN indicates that the iron is singeing the shirt.*)
>
> Oh, look at that. It's his best shirt.

IAN: It doesn't matter.

SHARON: Look at it.

> (*She starts to cry.*
>
> *IAN is embarrassed.*)
>
> I'll have to try and get him another.
>
> (*IAN turns back to the television.*
>
> *SHARON continues ironing.*)

Scene 8

The bedroom.

BARRY is lying on the bed. IAN enters with mug of tea. He stands looking at BARRY for a moment wondering what he will look like when he's dead. He goes to put the mug down and BARRY catches him doing it.

BARRY: What you doing?

IAN: Brought you a cup of tea.

BARRY: Oh.
> (*BARRY sits up and takes the tea.*
> *IAN backs off.*)
> What time is it?

IAN: Seven.
> (*IAN stands looking at BARRY wanting to go but unable to do so. Pause.*)

BARRY: Nice cup of tea. Thanks.

IAN: That's okay.

BARRY: What's your Mother doing?

IAN: Don't know.
> (*Pause.*)

BARRY: Going out tonight, are you?

IAN: Yes.

BARRY: Where you going?

IAN: Out.

BARRY: Someone special, is it?
> (*IAN gives him a questioning look.*)
> What's her name?

IAN: What?

BARRY: What's her name?

IAN: Whose name?

BARRY: The girl.

IAN: I'm going out with Lucy and Jeff.

BARRY: Oh, Lucy. Well, don't do anything I wouldn't do. Or if you do, be careful, eh?

IAN: Yeah.
> (*Another awkward pause.*)

BARRY: Nothing but trouble, that car.

IAN: What?

BARRY: The car. Nothing but trouble.

IAN: Yeah.

BARRY: Got a nasty feeling the drive shaft is going.

IAN: Expensive?

BARRY: Could probably get a second-hand one from a scrap
yard for fifty quid.

IAN: What about a new car?

BARRY: New car? Can't afford that, son.

(*Pause.*)

You mustn't be late. You don't want to keep her waiting.

IAN: No.

(*Pause.*)

Bye, then.

BARRY: Bye, son.

(*IAN turns to go.*)

Oh, Ian, get me a refill for this.

(*IAN hasn't seen him.*

He goes.)

Ian? Uhhh. Sharon. Sharon?

(*He bangs on the floor.*)

Scene 9

Bus stop.

IAN, LUCY and JEFF waiting for a bus. Sound of traffic.

LUCY: One coming?

JEFF: No.

LUCY: Says on the timetable they're every eight minutes.

IAN: (*Laughs.*) <u>Feee.</u>

JEFF: Perhaps we should hitch.

(*IAN and LUCY take up a signed conversation.*

JEFF is bored.)

IAN: <u>Saw Terry on Monday.</u>

LUCY: <u>Terry who?</u>

IAN: Terry Maxwell.

LUCY: <u>He's deaf?</u>

IAN: <u>Yes. Red curly hair.</u>

LUCY: <u>Do I know him?</u>

IAN: <u>Yes. He's always in the deaf club.</u>

LUCY: <u>I remember.</u>

JEFF: Look at this.

LUCY: (*To IAN.*) <u>Haven't seen him for years.</u>

JEFF: Luce.

LUCY: What?

JEFF: Yuppie coming along in his Toyota. Here, mate, give us
a lift.

(*They watch the car go by.*
IAN strokes his nose at the man.)

He's parking. We could go and nick it.

LUCY: Yeah, very funny.

IAN: What?

LUCY: (*Signing and speaking.*) He says we could steal it.
(*IAN smiles at JEFF.*)

JEFF: Thought you two would be into that. Seeing as how you
used to go shoplifting together.

LUCY: <u>What's Terry doing now?</u>

IAN: <u>He works at the swimming baths.</u>

LUCY: <u>Good job.</u>

IAN: <u>And he's getting married.</u>

JEFF: Ian?

LUCY: <u>Who's he marrying?</u>

IAN: <u>Don't know.</u>

JEFF: Ian?

IAN: What?

JEFF: Perhaps your Dad will come along in his XR3i.

IAN: Yeah.

LUCY: <u>She deaf?</u>

IAN: <u>Who?</u>

LUCY: <u>The girl Terry's marrying.</u>

IAN: <u>Yes.</u>

JEFF: Here's one.

(*He puts his hand out.*)

LUCY: It's only going as far as the Green.

JEFF: Awwwhhh. (*He waves the bus on.*)

IAN: (*To JEFF.*) What time we leaving on Monday?

JEFF: Hey?

LUCY: What time we going to Margate Monday?

JEFF: 'Bout eleven.

LUCY: <u>You asked your Mum yet?</u>

IAN: <u>Yes.</u>

LUCY: <u>Can you come?</u>

IAN: <u>Yes.</u>

LUCY: <u>Great.</u> (*To JEFF.*) He can come Monday.

JEFF: Great. (*He repeats her sign.*)

LUCY: <u>You been to Margate before?</u>

IAN: <u>No. I'm looking forward to it.</u>

JEFF: Right, see if I can tell you the make of every car.

LUCY: <u>Me too.</u>

    (*They continue signing.*)

JEFF: Okay?

IAN: What?

JEFF: I'll say the make of every car coming along. Bedford
    Van, Metro, Ford Cortina Estate, Volkswagen Golf.

IAN: Ford Fiesta.

JEFF: It's a Golf.

    (*Watches it go past, looks at the make.*)

IAN: Fiesta.

JEFF: You're right. Escort. Ummm, uhhh, ohhh, what is it?

IAN: Datsun.

LUCY: He's better than you.

JEFF: Your Dad tested any cars lately?

LUCY: Shut up.

IAN: What?

JEFF: What sort of car's your Dad got?

    (*IAN doesn't respond.*)

    XR3i wasn't it?

LUCY: Leave him.

JEFF: Funny, 'cause Luce thought it was an Austin Allegro.
    She says your Dad's not a test driver. He's a lorry driver.
    Hardly Alain Prost, she says. Going bald and got a beer
    gut, hasn't he? Now, this is a Golf and another Metro.

IAN: <u>What have you been saying about my Dad?</u>

LUCY: <u>Nothing.</u>

IAN: <u>You have.</u>

LUCY: <u>He has got a beer gut.</u>

IAN: <u>Shut up about my Dad.</u>

JEFF: Touchy.

LUCY: <u>What's wrong with you?</u>

IAN: <u>Nothing.</u>

LUCY: <u>You sure?</u>

IAN: <u>Yeah. I'm going to the shop.</u>

LUCY: <u>The bus might come.</u>

JEFF: Where's he going?

LUCY: Shop.

IAN: (*To JEFF.*) Want anything?

JEFF: Get me a can of coke.

LUCY: I'll have one too.

JEFF: Here's some money.

IAN: No.

JEFF: I'm working, you're not.

IAN: No.

   (*He goes.*)

LUCY: Don't go on at him.

JEFF: He shouldn't tell whopping great porkies.

LUCY: Just leave him.

JEFF: You should see the two of you. (*He mimics them doing sign language.*) I might as well not be there.

LUCY: Now you know what it feels like, then.

JEFF: Half the time I don't know what he's on about. (*He mimics IAN's voice.*) 'My Dad's a test driver.'

LUCY: Stop it.

JEFF: 'My Dad's got an XR3i.'

LUCY: Just cut that out.

   (*Pause.*

   They both look to see if the bus is coming.)

JEFF: I don't know why he has to go everywhere with us.

LUCY: He doesn't go everywhere with us.

JEFF: Coming to Margate, isn't he?

LUCY: He's me mate. I go out with you and your mates
   – Andy and Trevor and that Sue.

JEFF: That's different.

LUCY: You mean they're not deaf so it's me what gets left out.

JEFF: You manage alright.

LUCY: Lipreading's really hard, you know. Signing's a lot easier.

JEFF: Why don't you go out with Ian, then?

LUCY: And why don't you go out with that Sue?

(*Pause.*)

He's really looking forward to Margate.

JEFF: I know.

LUCY: I can't tell him you don't want him to come, can I?

JEFF: No. He can come.

LUCY: We'll have a laugh.

JEFF: Yeah. Here's the bus.

LUCY: Where's he got to?

JEFF: I'll go and get him.

LUCY: Quick!

(*JEFF goes.*)

(*To the bus driver.*) My mates are coming. They've just gone to the shop. (*Shouting to JEFF and IAN.*) Come on. (*To bus driver.*) They won't be a minute. Hey wait. They're coming. Wait. Owwwhhh.

(*The bus drives off.*

JEFF runs up.)

JEFF: You should have made him wait.

LUCY: He wouldn't. I think he said there's one behind.

JEFF: Awwhhh.

(*IAN runs up.*)

We missed it. It's your fault.

IAN: Sorry. Here. (*He gives JEFF the can.*) Lucy.

(*He gives her the other can.*

JEFF opens his can.

Because IAN has been running with it, it spurts out all over him.

IAN and LUCY try not to laugh.)

JEFF: Very funny.

(*IAN and LUCY burst out laughing.*

JEFF *starts shaking the can with his finger over the hole and*
advances on them.)
IAN / LUCY: No.
JEFF: I'll get you.
LUCY: Get off.
IAN: (*Pointing.*) Look, a Porsche.
JEFF: What?
LUCY: A Porsche. Look.
   (*JEFF looks around.*
   LUCY opens her can in his face.)
JEFF: You…
   (*He takes his finger off his can and it spurts over him again.*)
LUCY: Come on, the bus is here.
   (*They exit.*
   Sound of traffic.)

Scene 10

The hospital / the car.

BARRY and SHARON enter. BARRY looks ill and frail. He has a
small suitcase. They walk to the car and sit in it. SHARON drives
BARRY home.

SHARON: You okay?
BARRY: Feeling a bit sick.
SHARON: That's the treatment, though isn't it?
BARRY: Doctor said I might.
SHARON: That nurse seemed nice.
BARRY: Yeah. You have to turn left up here.
SHARON: I know.
BARRY: Indicate then.
SHARON: I am indicating.
BARRY: Oh.
   (*Pause.*)
SHARON: Lot of traffic. Everyone's going away for the
   weekend 'cause of the bank holiday.
BARRY: Mmmm.

SHARON: Tina's asked me to work in the betting shop Monday.

BARRY: Wants you to do her sums for her, does she?

SHARON: Ten till six-thirty. It's double time and a half.

BARRY: Mind this dustcart.

SHARON: What's he doing?

BARRY: Overtake.

SHARON: There isn't room.

BARRY: Go on.

SHARON: I can't. Oh, shut up. Bloke behind is flashing his lights.

(*BARRY leans over to her side to see if there is room.*)

BARRY: You'll get through.

SHARON: I don't think there's room. (*To the car behind.*) Will you shut up?

BARRY: Do you want me to do it?

SHARON: No. How near am I that side?

BARRY: Plenty of room.

(*She is edging forward trying to see if they can get through. BARRY tries to look her side.*)

SHARON: You look out that side.

BARRY: You're okay. Keep going.

SHARON: I know what I'm doing, Barry.

(*He looks out his side and jumps slightly towards her.*)

BARRY: Whoa.

SHARON: What?

BARRY: You knocked the wing mirror.

SHARON: You told me there was plenty of room.

BARRY: There was. You could get in closer your side.

(*Looking at the car behind.*) Stop blowing that horn. (*He shakes his fist.*)

SHARON: I've got six inches this side.

BARRY: (*Under his breath.*) Women drivers.

(*She goes to respond then says nothing.*)

SHARON: The dustcart's moving now, anyway.

BARRY: Thank the Lord for that. Let's get home before I throw up.

SHARON: Okay. So shall I tell Tina I'll do it? We could do with the money.

BARRY: I don't mind what you do.

SHARON: Ian'll be home. He can get your lunch. And I'll be back by seven.

BARRY: I said I don't mind.

Scene 11

The kitchen.

IAN is reading 2000 AD.

NARRATOR: 'Deep in the bowels of the undercity Judge Dredd and his weird companion have come face to face with Mortis.'

MORTIS: 'You cannot escape me, come.'

DREDD: 'Don't come any nearer creep.'

MORTIS: 'Your weapons cannot harm me. I am already dead. Hahahahaha.'
(BARRY enters.
They nod at each other.
SHARON enters.)

SHARON: Hello, love.

IAN: Hello.

SHARON: (*To BARRY.*) Wanna sit down?

BARRY: Think I'll have a lie down.
(He starts to go.
IAN watches him.)

SHARON: (*Unvoiced to IAN.*) He's feeling sick.
(BARRY turns and nearly catches them.
SHARON and IAN look at him.
He goes.
IAN goes back to his comic.
In the next sequence we see BARRY in the bedroom, sitting and then lying on the bed, IAN reading his comic and SHARON on the phone.)
Tina? It's me. I'm OK. Look, I'll be taking you up on that offer. I'll get to the shop for ten on Monday, shall I? Right.

(*BARRY starts knocking on the floor.*)

Hang on. Ian! IAN! Your Dad is knocking. Go and see what he wants.

IAN: (*Sighs exasperated.*) I'm fed up with this.

SHARON: Go on.

IAN: Uggh.

(*He goes to BARRY and then goes out.*)

SHARON: I don't know. I think he's alright. We just got back from the hospital. They said he had to rest. Oh, he looks terrible, Teen. I just wish there was something I could do. Sometimes think I make it worse. Well, they say it's stress, don't they, what causes it? Perhaps it's my fault he's got ill. Oh, I know. (*On the phone.*) Look I'd better go. Yeah, see you Monday. No, I'll try not to. Bye. Yeah bye.

(*IAN returns to BARRY with cigarettes.*

SHARON gets out vegetables, pan, saucepan and knife.

IAN returns to the kitchen.

BARRY gets a cigarette out, goes to light it, changes his mind.)

SHARON: What did he want?

IAN: Fags.

SHARON: He shouldn't be smoking.

(*IAN shrugs.*)

Here now you can help me with these carrots.

(*IAN frowns.*)

Come on. Here's a knife.

IAN: Carrots again.

SHARON: They're good for him. I'll scrape, you chop. (*They start work.*)

IAN: How far is it to Margate?

SHARON: How far is it to where?

IAN: Margate.

SHARON: Margate? Why?

IAN: I'm going there Monday.

SHARON: Monday? You can't.

IAN: What?

SHARON: I want you to look after your Dad on Monday.

IAN: No.

93

SHARON: Tina's got me some casual work in her betting office. They're short staffed Monday.

IAN: You promised.

SHARON: I don't remember.

IAN: You did.

SHARON: How you supposed to be getting there? Train?

IAN: Jeff's car.

SHARON: I'm not having you going off to Margate in a car with Jeff and Lucy. No knowing what sort of trouble you'll get into. You're chopping them too big.

IAN: You never let me do anything.

SHARON: What do you mean, I never let you do anything?

IAN: It's because I'm deaf.

SHARON: Don't be daft. Your hearing's got nothing to do with it.

IAN: You can't do that, you're deaf. You can't do this, you're deaf. I'm fed up with it. Lucy can do anything she likes.

SHARON: And Lucy's always in trouble. You were caught shoplifting because of her.

IAN: Long time ago.

SHARON: Anyway she's not as deaf as you.

IAN: You see. It *is* because I'm deaf.

(*Pause.*)

SHARON: You're selfish, do you know that?

IAN: What?

SHARON: Selfish. You're a selfish brat.

(*IAN looks away.*)

Listen to me. Your Dad's ill. Really ill. You got to help. I can't do it all myself.

IAN: I do help.

SHARON: You moan every time I ask you to do anything for him. I shouldn't have to ask.

IAN: But you said I could go. It's the bank holiday.

SHARON: Well, I'm sorry. I gotta take the work, we need the money. So you'll have to stay home.

(*IAN puts down the knife. He goes.*
SHARON looks at him.)

Scene 12

The betting shop / the house.

Sound of betting shop. Commentator at racetrack. SHARON is counting money and making a note of the amount. IAN is standing at a door of the bathroom where BARRY is being sick. After a while the commentator stops.

BARRY: This is supposed to be the cure. Oh God. (*He stops.*)
IAN: Okay?
BARRY: Think so. Can't be sick again. Nothing left in my
    stomach.
    (*He wobbles.*
    IAN holds him up.
    He puts his arm around IAN's shoulder.)
    Just get me back to bed.
    (*IAN helps him to the bed.*)
    Get me a drink of water lad.
    (*Looks questioning.*) Drink of water.
    (*IAN goes.*
    BARRY picks up a newspaper with a headline saying 'Head For The Beaches', tries to read, puts it down again.
    IAN returns. He sits on the bed, holds out the glass.
    BARRY brings his lips towards it. He helps him to drink.)
    Thanks son.
    (*IAN puts the glass down.*)
    What sort of day is it?
IAN: Hot.
BARRY: Mmm. Shame to be indoors. Your Mum get off
    alright?
IAN: Yes.
BARRY: Did she check the water? Don't want the car
    overheating.
IAN: I did it.
BARRY: Good lad.
    (*IAN picks up the paper. Sits beside the bed.*)
    That's Brighton Pier, isn't it? On the front?
IAN: What?

BARRY: Brighton.

IAN: Yeah.

BARRY: Your Mother and I used to go there bank holidays. On the motorbike. When we were courting. Remember the motorbike? We had it in the shed for years.

IAN: Yes.

BARRY: Those were the days. I was a Rocker.

(*IAN looks puzzled.*)

The Rockers had motorbikes and leather jackets. I had all the gear.

IAN: Mods and Rockers!

BARRY: That's right. Only the Mods had scooters – Lambrettas and Vespas – and wore suits and jackets and had daft haircuts. Used to be fights.

IAN: Did you fight?

BARRY: No, I used to try and keep out of it. Some went looking for trouble. Most of us just wanted a day out. Your Mum was in with a lot of Mods when I first met her. Your Gran didn't like me. She didn't want her little Sharon going out with a Rocker. She thought the Mods weren't as wild. Little did she know.

IAN: She was a Mod?

BARRY: Yeah, she was a Mod.

IAN: Why did she go out with you?

BARRY: She liked me I suppose.

IAN: How did you meet Mum?

BARRY: How did I meet her? Church Youth Club.

IAN: (*Laughs.*) You went to Church?

BARRY: Not me. Your Mum. But I went along to the Youth Club because I knew she went. Your Gran was very religious.

IAN: Still is.

BARRY: Yeah.

(*They both laugh.*)

Never could see the point in religion, myself. That's another thing your Gran has got against me. As far as I can see it, when you're dead, you're dead.

(*Pause.*)

IAN: Why did you get rid of it?

BARRY: Get rid of what?

IAN: The motorbike.

BARRY: When you came along we couldn't really use it any more.

IAN: I want a motorbike.

BARRY: You can't have a motorbike.

IAN: Why not?

BARRY: Too dangerous.

IAN: You had one.

BARRY: That was different.

IAN: Why?

BARRY: You don't want a motorbike, son.

IAN: What about a car?

BARRY: What about a car?

IAN: Can I learn to drive?

BARRY: You're not seventeen yet.

IAN: When I am seventeen. Will you teach me?

BARRY: We'll see.

IAN: Please.

BARRY: Don't go on about it, son.

> (*IAN is angry.*
> *BARRY watches him.*)

I'm hardly in any state to teach you to drive, am I? You always have to spoil things. I thought we were getting on really well an' all.

IAN: It's not fair. You're just like Mum. You won't let me do things. You had a motorbike but you won't let me have one. You won't teach me to drive.

BARRY: Here, not so fast. I thought they were supposed to be giving you speech therapy at that school. Still can't understand half of what you say.

IAN: Learn to sign. (*He signs it as he speaks.*)

BARRY: And you can cut that out. Talk properly. You won't get on unless you do. You gotta be able to communicate with people.

> (*Pause.*
> *IAN picks up the newspaper again.*)

If you're going to sit here and sulk I don't want you here.

IAN: I don't want to be here.

BARRY: Why are you here, then?

IAN: Mum told me I had to.

BARRY: Oh she did, did she? Well don't stay here just because your Mum told you to. I don't need you here. It's a sunny day outside. Get out with your friends. I'm sure they're doing something. Go on. What you waiting for?

IAN: What about your dinner?

BARRY: I don't want any dinner. Just leave me alone. I want to sleep.

(*IAN hesitates.*

BARRY turns away from him.

IAN goes.

BARRY lies still. Turns on a radio at his bedside.)

DJ: – is sunny and dry so today is going to be a real scorcher. For all you fun-loving people heading for the beaches here's a song from the late great Eddie Cochran.

(*The song 'The Summertime Blues' starts.*)

BARRY: Yeah, a bit of nostalgia.

(*BARRY lies listening to the song.*)

Scene 13

The street / JEFF's sar.

The song continues. LUCY gets into the car. Starts combing her hair, looking in the mirror. JEFF joins her and also looks in the mirror.

LUCY: Have we got everything?

JEFF: Think so.

LUCY: Money?

JEFF: Yeah.

LUCY: Map?

JEFF: Don't need one.

(*Music fades.*)

LUCY: We might.

(*IAN enters.*)

JEFF: What does he want? I thought you said he wasn't
coming.
(*LUCY turns.*)
LUCY: He isn't. Hello Ian.
IAN: Hello.
JEFF: Hello, mate.
IAN: Hello.
JEFF: We're just off.
LUCY: What's up, Ian?
IAN: Nothing.
LUCY: You sure?
IAN: Yeah. Can I come with you?
LUCY: To Margate?
IAN: Yeah.
LUCY: (*Looking at JEFF.*) I don't know.
JEFF: What's going on?
LUCY: He wants to come with us after all.
JEFF: You're joking! He can't now that we're staying the night.
LUCY: He could sleep in the car.
JEFF: Look, mate, we're staying overnight and going to a club.
Dancing – you wouldn't like it. It's not for kids.
LUCY: He's not a kid.
JEFF: (*Turning his back on IAN.*) Do you want to go to Margate
with him, or do you want to go with me? Make up
your mind.
LUCY: 'Course I want to go with you. But I thought…
JEFF: Well, think again. Two's company, three's a crowd.
LUCY: What'll he do?
JEFF: I don't know. I'm not his minder. I'll go and get the
map. Tell him, not this time.
(*He goes.*
Pause.)
LUCY : Sorry.
IAN: It's okay.
LUCY: I'll be home tomorrow night. Come round.
IAN: Maybe.
(*She goes to touch him.*
He pretends he hasn't noticed.)

IAN: <u>See you.</u>
LUCY: <u>Yeah.</u>
IAN: <u>Have a good time in Margate.</u>
LUCY: <u>See you.</u>
> (*He goes.*
> *She watches.*
> *Soundtrack of cars on a busy road.*)

Scene 14

A roadside.

The last verse of the Eddie Cochran song plays. IAN stands on his own. The sound of cars. He watches them. IAN has seen a car parked. He exits to steal it.

DJ: Yes. He's still one of the all time greats. Who knows what he'd have done if he hadn't had that fatal car crash in 1961. They say the good die young, don't they?
> (*The sound of cars continues.*
> *BARRY and SHARON enter.*
> *BARRY is lying on the bed.*
> *SHARON is looking out of the window.*
> *There is the distant sound of a siren.*)

Scene 15

The bedroom.

BARRY and SHARON. Pause.

BARRY: What time is it?
SHARON: Half twelve. You ought to get some sleep.
BARRY: I'm alright.
SHARON: Perhaps we should phone the police.
BARRY: Don't be daft.
SHARON: He's never stayed out this late. Didn't he give you any idea?
BARRY: I told you, I didn't ask him.

(*Pause.*)

I suppose you think this is my fault.

SHARON: No.

BARRY: You do. I can tell from that look on your face.

SHARON: Barry, I don't.

BARRY: Think I bully him, don't you?

SHARON: No.

BARRY: It's not me, it's you.

SHARON: What?

BARRY: You suffocate him.

SHARON: Was that a car? (*She goes to the window.*) No, it's just that lot over the road. Where can he be?

(*IAN is standing as if he is in a dungeon looking up.*)

NARRATOR: 'Judge Dredd is trapped deep under MegaCity. In the dungeons of Judge Death.'

DREDD: 'Let me out of here.'

JUDGE DEATH: 'Now I have you, Dredd. This time you won't escape. Soon you will experience the ultimate. Death itself.'

(*SHARON is making a cup of tea.*)

BARRY: For Pete's sake, he'll be back. At his age I was out on the streets all times of the day and night. My Mum didn't turn a hair.

SHARON: No, she was out boozing.

BARRY: She didn't mollycoddle me.

SHARON: Here, I've made you a cup of tea.

BARRY: I don't want any tea.

(*BARRY knocks the cup from her hand. The tea scalds her hand. She goes to get a cloth and kneels on the floor wiping the carpet.*)

Drives me bonkers the way you go on about him.

SHARON: Least I didn't wash my hands of him.

BARRY: Eh?

SHARON: Well, you did, didn't you? When you found out he was deaf.

BARRY: 'Course I didn't.

SHARON: Okay, you didn't.

BARRY: Couldn't get near him, could I? You made him into a Mummy's boy.

SHARON: You lost interest in him. I'll never forget it. We came back from seeing the specialist and you just said, 'You'll have to get a second opinion, won't you?' Not, 'we'll have to', 'you'll have to.' It was like you blame me.

BARRY: Don't talk rot.

SHARON: What is he?

BARRY: What do you mean, 'What is he?'

SHARON: What do you call people like Ian?

BARRY: Now what you getting at?

SHARON: People that can't hear, what do you call them?

BARRY: Deaf and dumb.

SHARON: Deaf. He's deaf. Not dumb. Because he speaks you see. And he's not stupid either. So he's just deaf. Perhaps if you'd gone to the specialist with him, just once, you'd know that.

BARRY: I'm working.

SHARON: You're his Dad. Then you wonder why you can't talk to each other.

BARRY: See, you do think it's my fault.

(*IAN sings words from the Eddie Cochran song.*
BARRY and SHARON sit still and quiet.)

IAN: 'I'm gonna take two weeks' (*Etc.*)

(*He sings the last four lines quietly underneath SHARON's speech.*)

'Sometimes I wonder' (*Etc.*)

SHARON: I can't help it. It's like he's part of me. I can't bear the thought of people laughing at the way he speaks or having one over him because he's deaf.

(*IAN goes.*)

What if something's happened to him and he can't make himself understood?

(*The phone rings.*)

BARRY: Go on.

SHARON: Hello? Yes, speaking. Yes… Yes, what's happened? (*A long pause.*) I see. That's very kind you. No, you're very near. Turn left after the High Street and keep

going. Clarendon Street's the third on the left and we're
number forty-five. Alright. Yes. Thank you.

(*She puts the phone down and returns to the bedroom.*)

BARRY Well?

SHARON: He's alright. He stole a car. The police picked him
up on the Ring Road this afternoon.

BARRY: This afternoon? Why didn't they get in touch before?

SHARON: 'Cause he wouldn't talk to them. He wouldn't tell
them where he lived or anything. Just said he'd run away
from home. They had to call in a social worker. That's who
that was.

BARRY: Where is he now?

SHARON: They released him into her care. In the end he
gave her his name and address. She's bringing him back.
They'll be here any minute.

BARRY: Thank Christ.

(*For the first time BARRY shows how worried he was.*
Pause.)

SHARON: Barry, I'm sorry.

BARRY: Your hand alright?

SHARON: Yes. I didn't mean all that.

BARRY: No, you're right. We can't talk to each other.

SHARON: You can –

BARRY: He hates me, Sharon, doesn't he?

SHARON: 'Course he doesn't.

BARRY: My own son hates me. You don't know what that
feels like. It hurts me…specially since…since all this.
I can't take it. I look at him, and he's looking back at me.
So cold. And it's too late now, isn't it?

SHARON: Too late for what?

BARRY: Too late to…to get to know him, I suppose.

SHARON: Course it isn't.

BARRY: I'll die and he won't feel a thing.

SHARON: You're not going to die. You're going to get better.

BARRY: Hold me, Sharon.

(*SHARON lies on the bed and takes him in her arms.*
Pause.
IAN appears at the doorway and watches them.

Pause.
BARRY looks up and sees him.)
Hello, son.
(SHARON looks around.)
IAN: The social worker's downstairs. She wants to talk to you.
SHARON: Alright, I'll go and talk to her.
(SHARON goes.
IAN looks at his father and starts to go.)
BARRY: Don't go son. Come and sit down.
(IAN sits reluctantly.)
You alright, lad?
(IAN doesn't respond.)
Why did you do it? Where did you think you were going? Eh? Margate? That where you were off to? Was it? Were the police alright? The police. Did they treat you alright? Look at me. I'm not going to shout at you. I want to understand. You'll have to learn to drive properly won't you?
(IAN looks at him.)
I said you'll have to learn to drive. I'll teach you. If I get better.
(IAN looks away again.)
Don't look away. Talk to me, son. I know it hasn't been easy between us two. But I do care about you, you know.
(IAN looks away again.
BARRY reaches out and touches him.)
Ian?
(IAN looks at him.
BARRY puts his fist to his chest and signs.)
I'm sorry.
Now how does it go?
You –
(He points at IAN.)
– must help – *(He signs help.)* – me.
(He points at himself.
IAN looks at him for a moment.
IAN starts to cry.
BARRY puts his arm around him.
IAN sobs.)

Scene 16

Living / dining room.

The mood of the previous scene is broken by Eddie Cochran singing 'C'mon Everybody'. SHARON is putting on her make up getting ready to go out. After a while BARRY and IAN enter. IAN has a bag with masks of horrific characters from 'Judge Dredd' stories. They put them on. SHARON switches the music off and turns round. They try to frighten her. She jumps and then ignores the masks.

SHARON: Well?
> (*BARRY shakes his head sadly.*)
> What did the solicitor say?
> (*IAN mimes cutting his throat.*)
BARRY: He's for the chop.
SHARON: They're pressing charges?
IAN: Twelve months in prison.
SHARON: Twelve months.
> (*She sits down.*
> *IAN and BARRY look at each other.*)
> You're having me on.
> (*IAN and BARRY laugh.*)
> Well, I don't think it's very funny. We got a court case
> hanging over us and a social worker coming and sticking
> her nose into our affairs. Doesn't make me want to laugh.
BARRY: The case is still with the Juvenile Bureau.
SHARON: They've had it for weeks.
BARRY: They have to decide whether they're going to press
> charges. But the solicitor has talked to them and she thinks
> she might be able to persuade them to drop it.
> (*BARRY goes to look at the record.*)
> Where did you dig this up from?
SHARON: I was in the shed getting out my old bike. Thought
> I'd use it to go to work on. I found a stack of your old 45s.
BARRY: Remember this one?
SHARON: Yeah. That's why I was playing it.
> (*BARRY puts the record on again.*
> *SHARON is looking in the mirror.*)

BARRY pretends to comb his hair like a rocker. He tries to get
SHARON to dance.)
Get off Barry. I'll be late.
BARRY: We used to clear the floor with our jiving.
SHARON: People were scared of getting trampled underfoot.
IAN: What?
BARRY: Come on. Show him.
SHARON: I've forgotten how to do it.
BARRY: Don't believe you.
SHARON: I have.
BARRY: Wasn't that long ago.
SHARON: Oh, alright.
(They dance a few steps.
IAN is left out.
BARRY gets hold of him and begins to show him the steps.)
Like this. That's it. Good.
(He signs.
BARRY suddenly feels very faint.
IAN and SHARON don't notice at first. They carry on dancing.
They see BARRY.
SHARON turns off the record player.)
You alright?
BARRY: Yeah.
SHARON: You mustn't overdo it.
BARRY: I'm okay.
SHARON: *(Signs over his head to IAN.)* Look after him.
IAN: Okay.
SHARON: Make sure he has a rest this afternoon.
(BARRY has seen this.)
BARRY: Make sure he has a rest this afternoon. Right?
IAN: Right.
BARRY: Getting good aren't I?
SHARON: Make sure you do.
BARRY: Me and my son have got something planned.
Haven't we?
IAN: What?
BARRY: We're doing something this afternoon.
IAN: Yes.

SHARON: What you doing?

IAN: (*Signs.*) <u>Secret.</u>

BARRY: Yeah. (*He signs.*) <u>Secret.</u>

SHARON: (*Taking a last look in the mirror.*) You behave
    yourselves.

BARRY: What time you got to be at work?

SHARON: Two o'clock. I'll be late.

BARRY: (*In a hearty way.*) What you want for dinner?

SHARON: Hey?

BARRY: We'll get your dinner.

SHARON: You don't have to.

BARRY: What you fancy?

SHARON: I don't mind.

BARRY: Pork chop?

IAN: Egg and chips?

BARRY: We got fish fingers from the shop.

IAN: And ice cream.

BARRY: Or would you rather have chicken?

SHARON: You choose.

BARRY: Chops it is, then.

SHARON: Bye then.

BARRY: Bye.

   (*He kisses her.*)

SHARON: Bye, love.

IAN: Bye.

BARRY: Don't be late back.

SHARON: I won't.

   (*She looks at him, then goes.*
   BARRY sits down looking dejected.
   IAN looks at him.)

BARRY: She's the breadwinner now.

   (*IAN doesn't understand.*)

   She earns the money now.

   (*IAN understands.*
   BARRY stays sitting.
   IAN goes and gets the car keys. Dangles them.)

   Hmmm? (*He brightens.*) Yeah.

IAN: Can Lucy come with us?

BARRY: Lucy wants to come?

IAN: Yes.

BARRY: Why not? The more the merrier.

> (*The music starts again – 'C'mon Everybody'.*
> *BARRY takes the keys from IAN. Puts his coat on. Looks at IAN*
> *and hands him the keys.*)

Scene 17

The car / Bisley Aerodrome.

The music continues through this scene but fades to a lower level during
the dialogue. LUCY is in the back. IAN driving. Throughout the scene
BARRY is talking but is also trying to sign.

BARRY: Okay, that's fine. Good. Good.

> Keep on the runway, keep on the runway.
>
> Straight ahead, straight ahead.
>
> Not so fast, Ian.
>
> Ian, not so fast.
>
> Slow down. Slow down.
>
> (*The song plays some more.*)
>
> Okay, change gear. What you doing? Change gear, I said.
>
> Change gear.

LUCY: (*Taps IAN on the shoulder and signs.*) Change gear.

BARRY: Okay.

LUCY: Don't distract him.

> (*IAN tries to sign to LUCY.*)

IAN: Change up or change down?

BARRY: Keep both hands on the wheel.

LUCY: Change up or down?

BARRY: (*To IAN.*) Down.

> (*IAN looks at him.*)
>
> Stop.
>
> (*IAN stops the car.*)
>
> You've got to keep your eyes on the road.

IAN: I can't understand you.

BARRY: I'm signing, aren't I?

IAN: You told me to turn the wheel.

BARRY: What?

LUCY: You said 'turn the wheel' not 'change gear.'

BARRY: Awwhh, I'll never get the hang of this.

> (*The song starts to fade up.*)
>
> This'll be the death of me. It'll be a heart attack what gets me in the end.
>
> (*He hasn't signed this.*)

IAN: What?

BARRY: Nothing. Keep your eyes on the road.

> (*IAN drives.*
> *The song continues and fades down.*)
>
> Okay, that's very good. Now let's try a three-point turn.

IAN: I want to drive round one more time.

BARRY: I'm the teacher. I tell you where to go.

IAN : No.

LUCY: (*Signing.*) <u>Do what he tells you.</u>

IAN: <u>You shut up.</u>

BARRY: Three-point turn.

IAN: No.

BARRY: You're impossible.

IAN: You're bossy.

BARRY: I'm not bossy.

IAN: Yes you are.

BARRY: You won't be able to argue with the examiner.

IAN: Don't care.

> (*The music fades up again.*
> *They continue arguing.*
> *But we can't hear them because the music is so loud.*
> *They stop arguing and all three look through the windscreen.*
> *The music fades completely.*)

SLEEPING DOGS

Characters

HAMIDA
a Muslim woman in her forties

ASSAN
her younger son

SEFAT
her older son

BORISLAV KAVIC
a Christian man in his forties

MARINA
his daughter

IRMA
a Muslim woman in her sixties

NADJA
a Muslim woman in her twenties

SABINA
a Muslim woman in her thirties

*The play is set in a side street of a small town facing a small
public garden.*

The time is the early 1990s.

Sleeping Dogs was first performed on 18 September 1993 by Red Ladder Theatre Company. The cast included:

MARINA, Jane Louise Arnfield

HAMIDA, Karen Bradley

BORISLAV, William Elliot

ASSAN, Karl Haynes

SEFAT, Tony McBride

Director, Philip Osment

Designers, Ali Allen and Marise Rose

Musical Director, Dave Crickmore

Scene 1

The street of a small town. Sound of birdsong and children playing.

HAMIDA is sitting on a chair outside her house grinding coffee. She stops and holds her face towards the sun with her eyes closed. SABINA appears at her window and looks at the statue. She is kneading dough in a bowl with flour.

HAMIDA: Lovely day.

SABINA: Soon be summer.

    (*IRMA enters. She is carrying two large shopping bags.*)

IRMA: They're not here yet then.

HAMIDA: No.

    (*IRMA continues. She goes to sit on her doorstep.*)

    You been shopping, Irma?

IRMA: Eh?

HAMIDA: I thought all the shops would be closed today.

IRMA: Not all of them.

HAMIDA: It will take you a long time to eat all that on your own. You're not getting married, are you? After all these years.

IRMA: I'm stocking up.

    (*HAMIDA and SABINA exchange looks and smile.*
    NADJA runs on and looks at the statue.)

NADJA: I thought I might be too late.

IRMA: Just got up?

NADJA: She's started.

IRMA: They spoil you,
    Your aunt and uncle.

    (*NADJA ignores her and goes and sits on HAMIDA's doorstep.*)

NADJA: I didn't want to miss it.

    (*They all look at the statue.*)

ALL: Today he's going.

NADJA: The leader.

HAMIDA: He's stood there for nearly fifty years in that little park.

NADJA: Call that a park!

   Patch of dusty ground with a plum tree.

ALL: Where the stray dogs sleep in the sun.

SABINA: For nearly fifty years he's stood over us.

NADJA: Watching us.

IRMA: His shadow falling on us.

ALL: And today he's going.

NADJA: In the capital today,

   Big events.

   Celebrations in St Peter's Square.

SABINA: A new government.

HAMIDA: So today all the statues of the old leader have
   to go.

IRMA: It's high time he went.

NADJA: Good riddance.

   (*She reads her magazine.*)

HAMIDA: What are you reading, Nadja?

NADJA: There's an article in here

   About the houses of the stars in Beverly Hills.

IRMA: Beverly who?

HAMIDA: It's an article about where the film stars live in
   Hollywood, Irma.

NADJA: 'This elegant bathroom belongs to a Warner Brothers
   mogul

   It has two porcelain baths,

   Two bidets,

   And three washbasins.

   Complete with gold taps.'

   Your husband, Hamida,

   Does he live somewhere like that in Germany?

HAMIDA: He shares one room with other guest-workers. It's
   another world.

IRMA: Gold bath taps.

   You live in a dream world, Nadja.

SABINA: Time you were married.

NADJA: Who's there to marry in this town?

SABINA: Have you seen my daughter, Hamida?

HAMIDA: She was there under the plum-tree.

Playing with that little Christian girl.

They went to the Square I think.

SABINA: She's not supposed to play in the Square.

IRMA: You worry about that child too much, Sabina.

SABINA: What does she know about having children?

IRMA: What did she say?

HAMIDA: Go and put your shopping away, Irma.

Then we'll sit down and have some coffee.

IRMA: Some coffee?

HAMIDA: Yes.

IRMA: Well –

HAMIDA: Don't worry, I'll treat you.

(*IRMA puts her bags indoors.*

HAMIDA goes to put the coffee on.)

NADJA: Look at this Sabina,

Michelle Pfeiffer's dining room.

(*HAMIDA returns.*)

HAMIDA: They're coming.

Irma!

They're bringing the crane up the street.

(*They all crowd forward to see.*)

NADJA: They're going to lift him off his pedestal,

SABINA: Put him on a lorry,

IRMA: And drive him away.

ALL: Change is in the air.

NADJA: Things can start happening around here now.

IRMA: So long waiting for this day.

SABINA: My child will have chances I never had.

HAMIDA: But will old wounds be opened?

ALL: Change.

You can smell it.

HAMIDA: It was time for him to go

But still…

IRMA: What?

HAMIDA: For fifty years we've lived in peace with our

Christian neighbours.

IRMA: For fifty years we've been forced to forget the past.

SABINA: Going to their door to borrow some honey.

IRMA: The leader gave them our houses and land.

NADJA: Watching their TV when our set was broken.

IRMA: And we rubbed shoulders with our enemies.

HAMIDA / NADJA / SABINA: Celebrating together
    Their feast days and ours.

HAMIDA: Today we should remember that.

IRMA: I remember when gunshots rattled down these streets,
    When we Muslims fought the Christians,
    And the dogs ate the corpses rotting in the street.
    (*Pause.*)

SABINA: They're tying ropes to the statue.

NADJA: Wrapping him up like a package.

HAMIDA: A parcel of history.

NADJA: My grandfather was tortured to death by Christians.

HAMIDA: At least the leader stopped all that.

SABINA: Things are different now.
    My child plays in the street with a Christian girl.
    It couldn't happen again.

HAMIDA: Not if we don't let it.

IRMA: It's already happening, Hamida.

SABINA: Don't talk about what's happening in the North!
    (*Pause.*)

NADJA: Look,
    They're attaching the ropes around the statue
    To the cable from the crane.
    It reminds me of that advert for jeans.

IRMA: What's she talking about now?

NADJA: I saw it at the cinema.
    There's this huge statue
    And they make some jeans for it
    And they pull them on with ropes.

IRMA: Trousers on a statue!
    (*They look at the statue.*)

ALL: Stories from the North.

HAMIDA: Rumours.

IRMA: All true.

ALL: Our people

Driven out of their homes by Christian militia.

SABINA: If that should happen here…

NADJA: It won't happen here.

HAMIDA: It mustn't happen here.

NADJA: We're in the majority here.

In the North the Muslims are outnumbered.

IRMA: The Christians who are here want our land,

And the Christians in the North will help them get it.

HAMIDA: We must hope and pray that you're wrong.

IRMA: We'll need more than prayers to protect us.

HAMIDA: You mustn't think the worst of people, Irma.

IRMA: Don't tell me what to think.

Always pretending to be so good.

SABINA: She is good.

NADJA: A good Muslim.

IRMA: Who never goes to mosque.

NADJA: The money her husband sends from abroad,

She gives half of it away to the poor.

IRMA: Better she used it to buy guns and ammunition.

She doesn't see the fight ahead.

You've always been too fond of Christians.

HAMIDA: You don't have children, Irma.

We don't want to see our sons and daughters lying dead

In a ditch.

SABINA: Don't talk like that!

You frighten me.

(*Pause.*)

NADJA: Look at him.

That's where he belongs,

On the end of a rope.

Where are your secret police now, Mr Leader?

We shouldn't quarrel,

Not today.

We should be celebrating.

SABINA: You always were a pessimist, Irma.

I remember how you used to say

That the dam they built above the town

Would crack and drown us all.

And yet it never happened.

NADJA: (*Quietly.*) She's scared of travelling to the capital.

She thinks the bus will crash.

HAMIDA: Shhhh.

IRMA: I can hear you.

NADJA: (*Quietly.*) She wants us all to ride on horses and carts.

IRMA: We may yet need our horses and carts.

NADJA: I'm going to travel in a supersonic jet.

And see New York before I die.

SABINA: Listen to her,

New York!

NADJA: Broadway,

Greenwich Village

Times Square.

ALL: The Statue of Liberty!

(*They look at the statue.*)

HAMIDA: They're putting him on the lorry.

IRMA / NADJA / SABINA: The ropes strain and slip.

NADJA: If they're not careful he'll fall.

IRMA: Let him fall.

SABINA: Smash on the dusty ground.

NADJA: Look, he is, he's falling.

ALL: Dust to dust.

Hurray.

(*They throw their arms up – SABINA's flour floats in the air like dust.*)

Scene 2

BORISLAV enters singing.

BORISLAV: 'The people's flag is deepest red

It shrouded oft our martyred dead

And ere their limbs grew stiff and cold,

Their heart's blood dyed its every fold.'

(*MARINA enters carrying his jacket.*)

MARINA: Father, come home, please.

BORISLAV: I'm coming, I'm coming.

Today's a special day you know.

The new government is being sworn in.

MARINA: I know.

BORISLAV: So, I'm entitled to celebrate.

MARINA: Come home and eat something first.

BORISLAV: Who knows?

We might not have a lot to celebrate when the fighting starts.

MARINA: Don't say things like that.

BORISLAV: Here's to you, my leader.

(*BORISLAV raises his bottle to toast the statue. He stops and looks around in mock confusion.*)

Where are we?

MARINA: What do you mean?

BORISLAV: Are we in the street with the plum tree?

MARINA: You know we are.

BORISLAV: I thought I was drunker than I am for a minute.

MARINA: They've taken the statue away.

BORISLAV: You have to keep your wits about you in this town nowadays.

Things change that quickly.

Statues disappear into thin air.

(*Sings.*) 'The people of this land

Once lived in poverty and war

The leader brought us peace

He gave hope to the poor.'

MARINA: Father, shhh.

BORISLAV: Why 'shhh'?

MARINA: People won't like hearing that song. Especially today.

BORISLAV: See what I mean?

The children used to sing that song every day at school.

Now it doesn't exist any more.

Phhht.

MARINA: Please, come home.

BORISLAV: What's the hurry?

MARINA: Your dinner's ready.

BORISLAV: You come and take me away from my friends in
    the café
    On this very special day in the history of my country
    When statues disappear
    And songs stop existing
    Just so my dinner doesn't get cold.
    (*He sings.*) 'He founded a republic here
    He ended civil strife.
    And enemies are comrades now.
    Let's build a better life.'
MARINA: Father!
BORISLAV: Do you disapprove of your old Dad so much?
    Do I embarrass you?
MARINA: Of course not.
BORISLAV: Do you want me to disappear too?
    Maybe if I stand here like the statue
    They'll come and cart me away.
    (*He takes up the pose.*)
    Am I still here?
MARINA: Yes.
BORISLAV: What a pity.
    I know what they call me.
MARINA: Who?
BORISLAV: The people in this town.
MARINA: They don't call you anything.
BORISLAV: Borislav the boozer.
    Hamida's son – what's his name?
MARINA: Assan?
BORISLAV: No, the other one.
MARINA: Sefat.
BORISLAV: That's him.
    He said it to my face the other day.
MARINA: He's just a layabout.
BORISLAV: A layabout in that family?
    Never!
    They're all so respectable.
    Not a drunkard among them.
    Their father slaves away as a guest worker in Germany

And sends back the money every month.

A nice hardworking little Muslim family.

Cheers!

MARINA: Shhh, they'll hear you.

We're standing right outside their house.

BORISLAV: That Assan's a clever boy.

He's going to be a doctor.

My star pupil

I did my best with Assan

But he'll still revert to the old ways in the end.

They're backward his family

The Imam governs their life.

MARINA: Assan doesn't even go to mosque.

BORISLAV: But his father does.

And soon he will.

They're fanatics.

MARINA: Father, I've made your favourite – goulash.

BORISLAV: They'll be making their women wear the veil soon.

MARINA: No one wears the veil here.

BORISLAV: Yet.

MARINA: Their Mother would never wear the veil.

BORISLAV: Hamida.

Hamida will do what they tell her to do.

She won't stand out against them.

MARINA: You've never liked Assan's mother.

BORISLAV: I don't trust her.

Hamida the saint!

She pretends to be everyone's friend.

Says we should all live together as neighbours.

Said it at the council meeting last week.

But she didn't say anything when they got rid of the mayor.

When is a mayor not a mayor?

MARINA: I don't know.

BORISLAV: When he's a Christian. Hah.

Good joke.

Hamida won't stick her neck out when there's trouble.

MARINA: There's not going to be trouble.

BORISLAV: Do you think she'll stand up to them when they
give me the sack?

MARINA: No one will give you the sack.

BORISLAV: The Imam won't want a Christian schoolteacher
Perverting the minds of the children.

MARINA: You're drunk.

BORISLAV: Me, who hasn't been in a Church for forty years.
Another joke.
Your poor mother tried so hard to get me to go to mass.
The rows we had about it.
Now they call me Christian.
Hah!
(*He takes another swig from his bottle.*)
This is the nearest I ever come
To taking communion.

MARINA: Shall I bring your bowl out?
You can sit out her and eat.

BORISLAV: I'm not going to sit and eat in the street with the
dogs.
The gossip that will cause:
'Did you see the schoolteacher eating his dinner in the
street?'
What an example to the young!
We should have moved back up North when your
mother died.
All my family live up there.

MARINA: This is our home.

BORISLAV: Now it's too late.
I'm too old to get a new job in the North.
We're stuck down here with all these Muslims.
(*She tries to put his jacket on him.*)
Leave me alone!
(*He pushes her so violently that she falls over.*)
You'd better convert to Islam
Wear the veil.
Then you'll be safe.
Find yourself a nice Muslim husband

To be your lord and master.

(*He drinks from his bottle.*)

MARINA: You brought me up to believe it didn't matter.

BORISLAV: Eh?

MARINA: Muslims, Christians we were all the same.

BORISLAV: I worry about you.

These are dangerous times.

MARINA: Nothing's going to happen to me

There's not going to be any trouble here.

BORISLAV: I love you, you know.

MARINA: I know.

BORISLAV: I don't know what I'd have done without you

In these years since your mother died.

MARINA: Father, come home.

BORISLAV: I know, I'm just a sentimental old drunk.

'Borislav the boozer', I know.

A laughing stock.

You've had a lot to put up with.

MARINA: Please don't.

BORISLAV: I was a disappointment to your Mother

And now I'm disappointing you.

MARINA: You're not.

BORISLAV: I am, I am.

You won't desert me, will you?

MARINA: You know I won't.

BORISLAV: Shhh. Give me your hanky.

(*HAMIDA and ASSAN enter carrying sacks.*)

HAMIDA: Good evening, Mr Kavic, Marina.

MARINA: Hello.

HAMIDA: Sefat will help you put them in the cellar, Assan.

Tell him to make sure the floor is dry.

(*ASSAN takes his sack indoors.*)

We managed to get the last two sacks of flour from the

miller.

Everyone has been buying,

They're worried stocks won't last.

BORISLAV: So they're all busy hoarding.

Every man for himself.

HAMIDA: Did you get any, Marina?

MARINA: No.

HAMIDA: You'll have to come to me if you run out.

BORISLAV: I thought you'd have been celebrating, Hamida.

(*ASSAN returns for the other sack.*

HAMIDA stops him taking it.)

HAMIDA: I'm not sure today is a day for celebration.

ASSAN: Don't be such a misery, Mother.

HAMIDA: Is Sefat there?

ASSAN: He said he's busy.

HAMIDA: Sefat! Can you come please?

BORISLAV: So aren't you pleased the statue's gone?

HAMIDA: He wasn't all bad the leader.

BORISLAV: You used to be his biggest critic.

HAMIDA: At least he brought us peace. Sefat!

BORISLAV: You went on the demonstration

When he tried to close down all the mosques and

churches.

HAMIDA: He was wrong about that.

BORISLAV: And the demonstrations

When he imprisoned all the leaders of the Peasants Party.

HAMIDA: That was wrong too.

He had his faults.

BORISLAV: But now you've got rid of him

You're sad to see him go.

HAMIDA: Things should change slowly.

Sefat!

BORISLAV: You should have thought of that

When you were doing all that demonstrating.

We might all live to regret those demonstrations.

(*SEFAT enters.*)

SEFAT: What is it?

HAMIDA: I wanted you to help put the sacks in the cellar.

SEFAT: I've got my new jeans on.

HAMIDA: I thought jeans were for working in.

SEFAT: These jeans cost me a lot of money

I'm not humping sacks in them.

HAMIDA: Assan can't manage on his own.

SEFAT: Oh, I forgot,
>   Your little Assan mustn't strain himself.

HAMIDA: He has to do his homework.

SEFAT: Got to save his strength, has he,
>   For reading his books?

HAMIDA: Please. Sefat.

SEFAT: So I have to do the donkey work.

HAMIDA: I'll help you, Assan.

SEFAT: Oh, now she's going to make me feel guilty.
>   She won't say anything
>   She'll just sigh and look sad.

BORISLAV: Let me help.

SEFAT: The state you're in
>   You'll fall down the stairs.

HAMIDA: Sefat!

SEFAT: We can manage without your help.
>   (*He picks up the remaining sack and goes indoors with ASSAN.*
>   *Pause.*)

HAMIDA: I'm sorry, Mr Kavic.

BORISLAV: Marina, my dear,
>   I think I left my book in the bar
>   I'll just go back and look for it.

MARINA: I'll go. You carry on home and eat your dinner.

BORISLAV: No, no. I won't be long.
>   (*They watch him leave.*)

HAMIDA: He's allowed his little drink today, my dear.
>   (*MARINA doesn't answer.*)
>   He put his faith in the leader and the party.

MARINA: I know.
>   All my life he's lectured me about it.
>   Now he won't admit that he was wrong.

HAMIDA: I remember your father,
>   When he was young,
>   Standing in the square
>   Urging people to join the party.
>   Electrifying his audience.
>   (*ASSAN returns.*)
>   He made us all believe that a new age was dawning.

An age of freedom and justice.

MARINA: But the leader put people in prison
If they didn't agree with him.
That's not freedom
Or justice.

HAMIDA: It didn't start like that.

ASSAN: Your generation got it wrong, Mother.
You must move over and let us run things.

HAMIDA: Maybe.
But don't be too hard on your father, Marina.
Today he saw his dreams die.
(*She goes.*)

MARINA: She's so good, your Mother.

ASSAN: Yes.

MARINA: She always stands up for father,
However rude he is to her.

ASSAN: Did you ask him?

MARINA: Ask who?

ASSAN: Your father.

MARINA: About what?

ASSAN: Stop teasing.
About you coming to the capital with me.

MARINA: You haven't got into medical school yet.

ASSAN: That's what you think.
(*He takes out a letter.*)

MARINA: You haven't.

ASSAN: I have.
(*She reads the letter and hugs him.*)
We'll find somewhere to live
In the old town.
My cousin will help me find a flat.
(*MARINA gives him back the letter.*)

MARINA: My father thinks there's going to be a war.

ASSAN: There's not going to be a war. Did you ask him?

MARINA: Have you told your Mother yet?

ASSAN: Plenty of time for that.

MARINA: So they still think you're going to marry the
butcher's daughter.

ASSAN: Amela?

MARINA: That's her.

ASSAN: She's still a child.

MARINA: With the body of a woman.

ASSAN: You're jealous.

MARINA: The way she looks at you.

ASSAN: It's you I want to be with.

(*MARINA doesn't respond.*)

Let's go to the hay barn.

MARINA: Now?

ASSAN: Yes.

MARINA: My father hasn't had his dinner.

ASSAN: Did you dream of me last night?

I dreamt of you.

MARINA: Lucky you.

I couldn't sleep.

ASSAN: Why not?

MARINA: I lay awake all night.

ASSAN: Thinking about us,

Together,

In the hay barn.

MARINA: If there's a war we couldn't go to the capital.

ASSAN: There's not going to be a war.

MARINA: It would be fun,

To live in the capital.

ASSAN: Yes.

MARINA: While you're at college

I'd get up late.

Then I'd get dressed in something really smart.

ASSAN: Oh yes?

MARINA: Then I'd go out and look in the shops

And buy myself a new dress

And some earrings

And maybe,

Have my hair dyed.

ASSAN: What then?

MARINA: Then,

I'd go and have my lunch

In a bar overlooking St Peter's Square.

ASSAN: And then?

MARINA: I'd spend the afternoon at the cinema
Watching the latest Tom Cruise film.

ASSAN: And then?

MARINA: I'd come home and make your dinner.

ASSAN: And then?

MARINA: You'd come home.

ASSAN: And then?

MARINA: We'd eat our dinner.

ASSAN: And then?

MARINA: We'd go out dancing.

ASSAN: And then?

MARINA: We'd come home again.

ASSAN: And then?

MARINA: Let me see…

ASSAN: Let's go to the hay barn.
Your father will be in the café for hours.

MARINA: Last night he asked me
Why there was a thistle in my hair.

ASSAN: My Mother found hayseeds in my socks.
And this morning,
I could still smell you
On my body
In my shirt.
I could hardly bear to wash or change my clothes.

MARINA: In the capital we'll be free,
Not like here –
Eyes watching all the time
Reporting back on us –
We'll do just what we like.

ASSAN: Are you coming?

MARINA: To the capital?

ASSAN: To the hay barn.
(*Enter SEFAT.*)

SEFAT: I thought you had homework to do, Assan.

ASSAN: I have.

SEFAT: You still here, Rabbit?

That's what we used to call her
At elementary school.
Remember?
MARINA: Yes.
ASSAN: What do you want?
SEFAT: Your teeth used to stick out
And you had bunches.
ASSAN: Stop it, Sef.
SEFAT: You've made up for it now though.
I could quite fancy you.
MARINA: I like your jeans.
SEFAT: American.
There's a shop in the City sells them now.
I could get you some next time I go.
MARINA: No thanks.
SEFAT: They're sexy, aren't they?
MARINA: That depends on what's inside them.
SEFAT: Always got an answer,
Haven't you, Rabbit?
MARINA: Remember what we used to call you?
SEFAT: (*To ASSAN.*) Mother wants you to go shopping.
MARINA: You always stank of garlic.
ASSAN / MARINA: 'Sef the Breath'.
SEFAT: You've got to get more bread and milk.
ASSAN: Why can't you go?
SEFAT: Because I have to go to the butcher's
To buy more meat.
Unless you'd rather go to the butcher's –
ASSAN: Mother's just been out to buy food.
SEFAT: We've got visitors coming.
ASSAN: Visitors?
SEFAT: Our cousins from the North.
ASSAN: What's happened?
SEFAT: They've walked over the mountains to get here.
ASSAN: All the way?
SEFAT: They couldn't get petrol.

Anyway,

The main road was being shelled.

So they walked.

ASSAN: Why did they leave?

SEFAT: They didn't want to get burned alive in their home.

That's what happened to the other Muslims in their village.

There's a war on up there.

MARINA: I'll see you later, Assan.

(*She goes.*

SEFAT pretends to point a gun at her.)

SEFAT: Run, Rabbit!

ASSAN: Leave her alone.

SEFAT: She didn't like hearing what her lot are doing to our people in the North.

ASSAN: They're not her lot.

She thinks what they're doing in the North is wrong.

SEFAT: What do you think the Christian army would do if they came here?

ASSAN: I don't know.

SEFAT: They'd put her Dad in charge

And put us into camps –

Can you imagine?

Borislav the boozer as head of police?

I'd rather die.

ASSAN: They won't come here.

SEFAT: Christian militia are in the area

Recruiting.

They've got training camps in the woods.

It's them or us.

So run, rabbit, run rabbit, run, run –

ASSAN: Don't call her that.

SEFAT: Why?

She's not your girlfriend is she?

ASSAN: Mind your own business.

SEFAT: She is.

Little Assan's got a Christian girlfriend.

ASSAN: Shut up.

SEFAT: Does she let you do it to her?

(*ASSAN doesn't respond.*)

SEFAT: Does she?

ASSAN: No.

SEFAT: Don't believe you.

You're not in love with her, are you?

ASSAN: Of course I'm not.

SEFAT: That wouldn't go down very well.

The butcher called on Mother the other day.

ASSAN: What for?

SEFAT: His daughter, Amela,

She'd make a good wife.

ASSAN: For you?

SEFAT: For you.

ASSAN: I'm going to college, Sefat.

In the capital

I'm going to be a doctor.

SEFAT: You'll do what you're told,

My little brother –

Remember,

I'm the head of the family

While father's away.

ASSAN: Father wants me to get qualified.

SEFAT: Okay, professor,

Just don't keep Amela waiting too long.

The butcher might find someone else for her to marry.

In the meantime,

Have your fun with Rabbit.

If you can bear the smell.

They all smell;

It's the meat they eat.

And I've heard she squeals like a pig when a boy gives

it to her.

(*ASSAN grabs him.*)

Alright, alright.

Hot under the collar, aren't you?

Go and let off steam with her.

(*ASSAN releases him and goes.*)

I'll write to father,

He won't let you marry her.

(*SEFAT sits down and takes out his gun. He looks at it. There is the sound of dogs growling.*

BORISLAV enters.)

BORISLAV: Be quiet.

(*He picks up a stone and throws it in the direction of the dogs. The growling ceases.*)

Going hunting?

SEFAT: Maybe.

BORISLAV: Pigeon?

SEFAT: Or rabbit.

BORISLAV: Your Mother's a good cook.

SEFAT: Mmmm.

BORISLAV: She's a good woman your Mother.

(*SEFAT doesn't respond.*)

That makes her difficult to live with.

SEFAT: You're not my teacher anymore.

(*Pause.*)

Coming sitting beside me

Breathing alcohol fumes all over me.

You stink.

You dirty old drunk.

Keep away from me.

Christian scum.

(*He goes.*

Sound of dogs growling.

BORISLAV looks at the dogs for a moment then leaves.)

Scene 3

Birdsong but no children. The sound of wood being chopped. HAMIDA sits outside her house. She pours coffee into a cup. IRMA looks out of her window. HAMIDA turns off the radio.

HAMIDA: There's a chill in the air today.

IRMA: Mmmmm.

HAMIDA: Winter's on its way.

(*They look out.*)

IRMA / HAMIDA: All summer we've held our breath.

IRMA: Fearing the worst.

HAMIDA: Hoping for the best.

IRMA: As the fighting got closer.

HAMIDA: Now we watch for the first snowflake.

IRMA: The first round of gunfire.

IRMA / HAMIDA: The winter will be hard.

IRMA: You still have coffee, Hamida?

HAMIDA: This is our last bag of beans.

IRMA: Thought I could smell coffee.

HAMIDA Here.

> (*IRMA brings her cup.*
> *HAMIDA pours.*)

IRMA: There hasn't been coffee in the shops for months.

HAMIDA: Not since the day they took the statue down.

IRMA: People hoard it, you know.

> (*HAMIDA looks at her. They drink.*
> *ASSAN passes them carrying chopped wood into the house.*)

No school today?

ASSAN: It's shut.

HAMIDA: He was supposed to be going to medical school this autumn.

IRMA: The men spend all their days chopping wood.

HAMIDA: The road to the city is mined.

IRMA: All the factories have closed anyway.

It's even dangerous to work in the fields.

HAMIDA: No need to sound so pleased.

IRMA: Eh?

HAMIDA: Nothing.

> (*Pause.*)

I've come to hate the sound of the axe.

IRMA: It gives them something to do.

HAMIDA: It's the sound of people waiting,

For history to roll over them;

Flattening what has been built

Crushing hopes

Squeezing goodness out.

(*ASSAN crosses back.*)

IRMA: At least we won't be short of firewood this winter. Eh, Assan?

ASSAN: No.

IRMA: You can bring some into me later.

Reminds me of the old days.

We always used to stock up with logs for the winter.

No use relying on the electricity supply.

(*The chopping has stopped.*

HAMIDA and ASSAN are listening.)

I'm glad I've still got my wood burning stove.

HAMIDA: Shhhh.

IRMA: When everyone threw their stoves out

And put in electric cookers

I kept mine.

HAMIDA: Quiet.

IRMA: What's happening?

(*Pause.*

They listen.

Distant gunshots.

ASSAN runs off.)

HAMIDA: A car exhaust.

IRMA: The road is empty.

HAMIDA: Thunder.

IRMA: There are no clouds in the sky.

HAMIDA: Firecrackers.

IRMA: The celebrations have stopped.

Those are your first thoughts when you hear such sounds in peacetime.

You have forgotten they can have more sinister causes.

But not me.

Fifty years of peace cannot wipe out the memory.

(*NADJA enters.*)

NADJA: The bus has been stopped.

That was taking the last children away from the town.

People are running down the road that leads to the river.

HAMIDA: Where is Sabina?

Her daughter was on that bus.

She waited and waited
But in the end she decided to send her away.

NADJA: She picked up the kitchen knife
And ran down the road
Her hands covered in flour.

IRMA: She still has flour?

NADJA: The men have run to fetch their shotguns
And their hunting knives.

HAMIDA: For fifty years they've served us well,
Those knives and guns.
Providing us with rabbit stew
And pigeon pie.

NADJA: The mothers are returning,
Carrying bundles.

HAMIDA: Bundles of rags.

NADJA: Dripping red.

IRMA: Bodies.

IRMA / NADIJA / HAMIDA: The bodies of their children.

(*SABINA enters with her child in her arms.*
The knife still in her hands.)

SABINA: Still warm,
She's still warm.
While I was measuring out the flour
She was sitting chatting to her friend.
While I was weighing out the butter,
Armed men stepped in front of the bus.
While I was mixing them together,
They shot the driver and got on board.
While I was adding sugar
They separated my daughter from her friend
Lined her up with the other Muslims on the bridge.
While I was cracking eggs
Someone held a knife to her neck.
While I was stirring them in,
He slit her throat.
As I poured the mixture into the tin
She died.
Feel her,

She's still warm.
(*She drops the knife onto the ground.*
They go to comfort her.)
Leave me.
(*She goes.*
NADJA follows.
A bell rings.)
HAMIDA: That's the Christian Church.
(*IRMA looks at her.*)
HAMIDA: They're ringing the bell.
IRMA: Why are they doing that at this hour?
(*Enter SEFAT.*)
SEFAT: We ran into the woods
        Following their tracks.
        But they had melted away into the trees.
        Here, some trampled bracken,
        There a discarded cigarette packet,
        But they were gone.
        We came upon a clearing,
        Their camp,
        Abandoned.
        Blood,
        Everywhere
        Carnage
        A stench to make you gag.
        Bodies
        All over the ground,
        Beneath the trees.
        At first we thought they were human.
        Then we looked closer.
        Pigs,
        Slaughtered pigs.
        Each one with a clean gash at the throat,
        Blood caked and brown on the dead leaves.
IRMA: Ah yes,
        I remember.
HAMIDA: What do you remember?
IRMA: That's how they always teach their new recruits.

They practise on pigs,
Rehearse how to kill us,
Using pigs.
Prepare to slaughter us like pigs.

SEFAT: Our neighbours.

They're our neighbours.

HAMIDA: No.

A band of irregulars from the North.

IRMA: Not all from the North.

There must have been some local men amongst them

How else would they know which were the Muslim
children?

SEFAT: They must hate us so much.

Why do they hate us so?

HAMIDA: Farmer Godac who is so kind to us is a Christian

And Doctor Melovic

And half the teachers at your school were Christian.

IRMA: They're not all bad.

But the good ones are more dangerous.

They are like sheep,

These good Christians,

Easily led.

Their leaders tell them we want their homes,

Their jobs,

Their lands.

We Muslims are wolves

Ready to devour them all

HAMIDA: They know that isn't true.

IRMA: But fear hides the truth from their eyes.

Fear is a weapon –

Being used against us.

A frightened people wants strong leaders,

So their leaders try to keep the Christians scared.

HAMIDA: Even now

We must believe

That the ordinary Christian wishes us well.

Even now,

We must hope that they will not be deceived
Into waging a war that will destroy us all.
IRMA: We must harden our hearts against them.
Do not see the friend who helped you with the harvest
See the thief.
Do not see the doctor who cured your daughter's illness
See the rapist.
Do not see the teacher who taught you how to read
See the child murderer.
They don't see us,
They see wolves.
Let us grow fangs and claws.
(*SABINA can be heard sobbing.*)
HAMIDA: I must go to Sabina.
(*She goes.*)
SEFAT: (*Calling after her.*) You fed me on the milk of human
kindness. It tastes sour to me now. I'm old enough for red
meat, Mother.
(*MARINA enters.*)
MARINA: Is Assan –
SEFAT: No.
(*IRMA goes to her house.*
MARINA turns to go.
SEFAT goes and stands in front of her.)
But I'm here.
(*She turns to go again.*)
Aren't you pleased to see me, little Christian girl?
You used to like me at elementary school.
(*He grabs her and tries to kiss her.*
She struggles.)
I thought you liked to be kissed.
You used to let me kiss you.
MARINA: I was a child.
It was a game.
SEFAT: Why don't you like me?
MARINA: Whenever I see you,
You stare at me.
Your eyes follow me around the town.

140

It makes my flesh creep.

SEFAT: It can't be because I'm Muslim.

Assan's Muslim.

MARINA: Is that all you can see?

A Muslim or a Christian?

SEFAT: Oh, I forgot.

Your father brought you up to think it didn't matter.

MARINA: Wars happen when people think it matters.

SEFAT: Yes,

Muslim children get killed,

By Christian militiamen.

(*Pause.*)

Do you want to kill a Muslim?

Here,

Take my gun.

Here,

Take it.

You pull the trigger like that.

Come on,

Now's your chance.

Here,

This is the best spot to put the muzzle.

This is where the bus-driver was shot.

Here,

Right on the temple.

Or would you prefer to use a knife?

(*He picks up SABINA's knife.*)

Look a nice soft throat.

Not as soft as a child's throat, I know,

Bonier

And tougher.

But you could do it.

Look,

I know you don't want to touch me

But isn't my bare throat just a little bit inviting?

Wouldn't you like to see the blood gush out?

Just one strong slash –

And I'm a dead man.

(He has been trying to get her to hold the knife.
It falls to the ground.)
Christians should be careful walking the streets tonight.
We might take our revenge,
One way or the other.
(He kisses her.
She goes.
IRMA is looking out of her window.)
IRMA: That would be the real test.
SEFAT: What?
IRMA: Then we'd really know what you're made of.
(HAMIDA enters.
She looks at them.)
Sabina won't open her door.
(Pause.
The sound of the mass can be heard in the background.)
HAMIDA: All the Christians are going to the Church
To say a mass for our dead children.
Do you hear that, Irma?
They're grieving with us.
Sefat,
Do you hear?
They're saying prayers for our dead.
(IRMA goes.)
What has she been saying?
(SEFAT doesn't answer.)
Was Marina just here?
She ran past me.
I tried to stop her.
(ASSAN enters.)
Where are the men?
ASSAN: They've set up roadblocks.
SEFAT: We want more than roadblocks.
We want revenge.
Are you coming, Assan?
HAMIDA: Leave him alone.
SEFAT: All my life I've lived with your goodness, Mother,
All my life it has made me feel bad.

Assan was the good son,
Assan was the clever one.
People in this town call me good-for-nothing
And whisper about me in doorways as I pass them in the street.
What use is your goodness now Mother?
Will it stop the slaughter?
This is Sefat,
The bad son,
The good-for-nothing,
His time has come.
(*He goes.*)

HAMIDA: Are you seeing Marina later?

ASSAN: No.

HAMIDA: Are you sure?

ASSAN: Of course.

HAMIDA: The hay-barn in your Uncle's orchard
Can be clearly seen from my bedroom window.
(*ASSAN doesn't respond.*)

HAMIDA: Are you meeting her there this evening?

ASSAN: We said we might.

HAMIDA: Go to her,
Find her,
Make sure she's somewhere safe.
Warn her to keep off the streets.
Tell her father to bolt all the doors and windows.
To be a Christian in this town tonight is a dangerous thing.

ASSAN: The Christians are just as outraged as us.
This will bring the town together.

HAMIDA: She must stay in tonight.

ASSAN: Sefat likes to talk but he wouldn't really hurt anyone.

HAMIDA: Do you remember his little dog?

ASSAN: Yes.

HAMIDA: The day I found him beating her with a stick.
I can see her now,
Cowering
Her tail between her legs

Her head bowed
Her belly near the ground
As the blows rained down on her back.
It sent a chill through me.
ASSAN: That was years ago.
HAMIDA: 'She wouldn't come to me when I called'
He told me.
'She went out in the fields with Assan.
She's my dog.
I called and called and she wouldn't come.
She's my dog.
She's my dog.'
ASSAN: What are you saying?
HAMIDA: Go quickly
Before it's too late.
(*ASSAN goes.*)
All may yet be well.
So many years looking over my shoulder,
Watching the neighbours' faces
As they looked at my child.
Could they tell?
Did they know?
Would the gossip reach my husband's ears?
But I was lucky
All was well.
The baby that I suckled
Drank in shame.
But all was well.
The toddler walking beside me down the street
Felt the guilt in my damp hand.
And all was well.
The schoolboy I told to work hard
Heard mistrust in my voice.
Still all was well.
The youth, lovesick for Marina,
Read horror in my eyes.
Then she chose Assan.
No incest in that.

All was well.

But my guilt poisoned my son.

Now the man spits it back at me as resentment and hate.

My luck is running out.

But all may yet be well.

(*BORISLAV enters.*

HAMIDA is startled.)

BORISLAV: Have you seen my daughter, Hamida?

HAMIDA: She was here.

Hasn't she come home?

BORISLAV: No.

HAMIDA: Perhaps she's at the mass.

They're saying prayers for the children who died.

BORISLAV: I've already looked there.

The priest nearly spilt the communion wine

He was so shocked to see me.

HAMIDA: Do you think it will all start again?

BORISLAV: I hope not.

HAMIDA: Oh, Borislav,

I'm so scared.

(*She moves to touch him.*

He stops her.

Pause.)

Have you been to the old hay barn?

BORISLAV: Why should I go there?

HAMIDA: You are so concerned about what is happening in

your country

But you miss what is happening in your home.

You were always so.

Your eyes were on the big events

And so you missed the small ones.

BORISLAV: What are you trying to tell me?

HAMIDA: That Assan and Marina meet there,

In the hay barn,

Just like…

BORISLAV: And you let this happen?

HAMIDA: Why shouldn't it happen?

BORISLAV: Can't you answer that question for yourself?

You have a short memory.

(*He starts to go.*)

HAMIDA: Wait here.

It's not safe for you to be on the streets tonight.

(*ASSAN returns.*)

ASSAN: There's no one at home.

BORISLAV: I could have told you that.

ASSAN: Where is she?

BORISLAV: Your Mother tells me I should ask you that.

HAMIDA: Not at the hay barn?

ASSAN: No.

I went to the church but she wasn't there.

(*BORISLAV goes.*)

HAMIDA: And Sefat?

ASSAN: What about him?

HAMIDA: Have you seen him?

ASSAN: He and some others are patrolling the town.

HAMIDA: Patrolling?

ASSAN: You know Sefat.

HAMIDA: What are they doing?

ASSAN: Mother!

HAMIDA: Tell me.

ASSAN: They've put red paint on the graves in the churchyard.

HAMIDA: And?

ASSAN: Broken the windows in Christian homes.

HAMIDA: Is that all?

(*NADJA enters.*)

NADJA: Hamida,

The town is going to be on television.

There are two foreign reporters –

They've asked me to be their guide.

One of them wants to talk to Sabina.

Do you think she'll do it?

HAMIDA: She can't.

NADJA: He's from CNN.

HAMIDA: Sabina needs to be left alone to grieve.

NADJA: But he's on our side.

 I've spoken to him.

 He wants to help us.

 If she goes on television,

 The world will hear her story.

 What they did to defenceless children.

 She's got to do it.

 It's her duty.

 He said a story like that can have a huge effect.

HAMIDA: A story?

 Is that what this is?

NADJA: They filmed Sefat and his friends out on patrol.

 (*She goes.*)

ASSAN: Sefat won't do anything, Mother.

HAMIDA: I hope you're right.

 (*BORISLAV returns.*)

BORISLAV: Where have they taken her?

ASSAN: Who?

BORISLAV: Tell me where they've taken her.

HAMIDA: Borislav.

BORISLAV: Some young men were seen dragging her up the

 street.

 Your son, Sefat, was with them.

 The priest heard her screams from the Church

 But, being a priest, did nothing to stop them.

 Where have they taken her?

HAMIDA: We'll help you find them.

BORISLAV: You must know where they've gone.

 The priest said you were there too.

ASSAN: Not me.

 (*BORISLAV picks up the knife, throws ASSAN to the floor,*
 pushing HAMIDA out of the way, and holds the knife to his
 throat.)

HAMIDA: Borislav!

BORISLAV: If anything has happened to Marina I'll kill you.

ASSAN: Sir.

BORISLAV: What?

ASSAN: It's me, Sir, Assan.

BORISLAV: So?

ASSAN: I love her.

BORISLAV: You love her?

    Love has no place in this town now.

    It's been carted away with the statues and the songs.

    You think that just by saying the word

    You can solve everything.

    Did you hear that, Hamida?

    He loves her.

    How much is his love worth?

    He thinks it will conquer all.

    We know it won't, don't we?

    Not when there's a father to be obeyed,

    Not when there's land to be inherited,

    Not when there's a holy man to be heeded,

    Not when the tribe says, 'No'.

HAMIDA: Put the knife down.

    The men are out looking for the irregulars

    Who killed the children on the bridge.

    If they return to find you holding a knife to his throat,

    They'll shoot you before you have the chance for a

    Second thought.

BORISLAV: Do you think I care what happens to me?

HAMIDA: Please Borislav,

    I beg you,

    Put the knife down.

    (*BORISLAV looks at her.*

    He drops the knife.)

BORISLAV: She's all I've got left.

    My life would be nothing without her.

    (*Enter SEFAT.*)

HAMIDA: Where have you been?

SEFAT: On patrol.

    (*He starts to go into the house.*)

BORISLAV: Where is my daughter?

HAMIDA: Answer him!

SEFAT: Your daughter?

Where is Sabina's daughter?

And Fatma's son?

And the Kasim twins?

Where are all the men

Who have been marched away to camps from villages in the North?

Where are all the families burnt to death in their homes?

(*HAMIDA slaps him.*)

HAMIDA: Where is Marina?

SEFAT: How would I know?

HAMIDA: What have you done to her?

ASSAN: He hasn't done anything, Mother.

SEFAT: Oh haven't I, little brother?

Maybe I've made her squeal –

Maybe she liked it when I did.

Maybe she thought I was better at it than you.

HAMIDA: No.

SEFAT: I raped her, Mother,

Then we executed her.

(*ASSAN runs at SEFAT. He holds ASSAN off.*)

Now you know what Sabina feels,

What Fatma feels.

What does it feel like, Mr Schoolteacher?

(*As ASSAN fights him, BORISLAV comes up behind SEFAT and stabs him with the knife.*)

HAMIDA: Borislav!

(*SEFAT relaxes his hold on ASSAN.*)

SEFAT: In the back

A blade.

Cold steel in the back.

Is that what it feels like,

The fatal blow?

Is this how death comes?

An unpleasant surprise?

While your brother fights you

And your Mother looks on?

(*HAMIDA is holding SEFAT.*)

HAMIDA: Run and fetch the doctor.

(*ASSAN looks at BORISLAV.*)

He won't harm me.

Go on.

(*ASSAN goes.*)

SEFAT: There, Mother.

Now you're rid of me.

Now you can have a quiet life, eh?

No more worrying about what that wicked son of your is up to.

HAMIDA: The doctor will be here soon.

SEFAT: Yes.

The doctor who comes to us all in the end.

No more pain

After a visit from him.

HAMIDA: Hold on.

SEFAT: For what?

More of the same?

It's like diving into a river,

This dying.

At first the shock takes your breath away.

But you soon get accustomed to the temperature.

Mother!

HAMIDA: I'm here.

SEFAT: I'm drowning.

Don't let me drown.

HAMIDA: I won't.

SEFAT: It wasn't easy. Mother.

HAMIDA: What wasn't easy?

SEFAT: What I did.

(*He dies.*)

HAMIDA: Sefat?

(*She keeps whispering his name in the hope that he isn't dead. Then she realises that it is useless.*)

Sefat!

Too hasty.

They're all too hasty

To reach for the gun and the knife.

Blade plunges into flesh,
Bullet splinters bone.
So easily.
So quickly.
You too, Borislav,
Too hasty.
Too hasty to kill what is yours.

BORISLAV: What are you saying?

HAMIDA: Did you never hear what they whispered about
him?
Did it never reach your ears?

BORISLAV: They said he was a good-for-nothing.

HAMIDA: Not when he was born.
Then they said he was a heavy baby to be two months
premature.
Some said he must have been conceived before my
marriage to Ali.

BORISLAV: I don't believe you.

HAMIDA: Look at him!
Do you not see the likeness?
Even as he taunted you
Did you not wonder why his eyes were blue
When the rest of his family has hazel eyes?
As you held the knife against him
Did you not notice
That his hair was fair like yours used to be
Rather than brown like my husband's and mine?
As you plunged the blade into him,
Did you not see the strawberry birthmark on the back of
his neck?
The mark that you have,
That Marina has.

BORISLAV: Your son was a rapist and a murderer.
He was never my son.
(*He goes.*)

HAMIDA: His smile was just like yours too.
May I be forgiven that he smiled so rarely.
(*She sings under her breath.*)

151

'Bye baby bunting
Daddy's gone a-hunting
He's gone to get a rabbit skin
To wrap my baby bunting in.'
(*ASSAN returns with bandages.*)
ASSAN: The doctor is at the hospital
 Tending the children wounded on the bridge.
 We must take him there.
HAMIDA: No doctor can help him now.
ASSAN: I'll carry him there.
 (*He is trying to pick SEFAT up.*)
 Help me, Mother.
HAMIDA: It's too late.
ASSAN: I can do it easily.
 (*They fight over the body.*)
HAMIDA: He's dead, Assan.
 (*ASSAN still doesn't believe her.*)
 He's dead.
 (*They look at the body.*)
ASSAN: If I hadn't been fighting him…
HAMIDA: Let's carry him indoors.
 (*ASSAN cries.*
 IRMA enters.)
IRMA: I've saved my horse from the Christian army.
 They're not having him.
 Christian militiamen are digging in on the hillside.
 (*She sees SEFAT's body.*)
 How did this happen?
 (*Pause.*)
 Who did it?
ASSAN: The schoolteacher. Borislav.
IRMA: Ahhhh.
 (*She looks at HAMIDA.*)
HAMIDA: Marina is dead.
 Sefat killed her. –
IRMA: Then I've just seen a ghost.
HAMIDA: What?
IRMA: Marina Kavic is alive.

HAMIDA: You must be mistaken.

IRMA: She's at the hospital.

    I saw her go in as I passed.

    She was speaking to a doctor.

    A Muslim doctor.

    I shouted at him not to treat her.

    He ignored me and led her away.

    How dare she go there

    Where our children are dying?

    Sefat may be dead, Hamida,

    But Marina is alive.

HAMIDA: He said he'd killed her.

    He told Borislav he'd killed her.

IRMA: He did it to make him suffer I'm sure.

HAMIDA: He said he wanted Borislav to feel what

    Sabina feels.

IRMA: He died in a good cause then.

HAMIDA: There is no good cause for this.

    Come, Assan.

ASSAN: Are you sure it was Marina that you saw?

IRMA: There's nothing wrong with my eyesight.

    What are you going to do?

HAMIDA: Help me, Assan.

IRMA: Are you going to let your brother's killer live?

HAMIDA: Don't listen to her.

IRMA: This is a fine mother.

    She sits there with her son's body in her arms.

    And wants to protect his murderer.

    Does Borislav mean that much to you still?

HAMIDA: I want to mourn my son.

IRMA: Is this the way you will mourn Assan when he dies?

HAMIDA: I still have hope.

IRMA: Hope?

HAMIDA: Yes, hope.

    That he will outlive me.

    It's natural for sons to outlive their mothers.

IRMA: None of us will survive

    If we sit back and let them slaughter us.

Is it natural for a mother to do that too?
HAMIDA: What would you know, Irma,
   About maternal feelings?
   What do you know of a mother's grief?
   You are childless.
   But you are eager to see other women's children sent to
   their deaths.
   You are jealous that I have sons,
   You want them dead.
   Take his feet, Assan.
IRMA: Take his gun
   And join the fight.
   (*ASSAN and HAMIDA carry the body away.*
   IRMA calls after them.)
   I was still a girl
   When it happened last time.
   But I remember it clearly,
   The night the soldiers
   Kicked in our door,
   Made my father watch as they raped my mother
   Made us watch as they castrated him.
   After they were dead the soldiers turned on me.
   A child cowering in the corner of the kitchen.
   When they had finished
   One of them took out his knife
   And put it inside me.
   'That should stop you breeding,' he whispered.
   They left me for dead on the bloodstained floor.
   He thought he'd made me barren
   But I conceived a child that night
   A child that I have carried in my belly for fifty years
   And today I give birth
   To the product of that union.
   Today my child emerges into the light.
   Begotten in hatred,
   His name is vengeance
   And his first cries will echo
   Through every Christian home.

(*Enter NADJA.*)

NADJA: Don't go into the Square, Irma.

IRMA: To the Square?

NADJA: Someone is firing from the teacher's house.

IRMA: From the house of Borislav?

NADJA: I was bringing the reporters back from the hospital

Suddenly bullets rained down on us.

A sniper must have broken into his home.

IRMA: How do you know it wasn't the teacher himself?

NADJA: Borislav wouldn't shoot at us.

IRMA: He has already killed Hamida's son, Sefat.

(*Pause.*)

NADJA: I'm scared, Irma.

The world's gone mad.

Borislav –

IRMA: What?

NADJA: He speaks five languages.

Reads poetry in French.

He went to London once on a conference.

IRMA: Now he's showing his true colours.

NADJA: But he taught all our children.

IRMA: Now he's trying to undo the work

By killing them.

NADJA: My reporter says he may be able to get me out.

If he can,

I'll go with him.

I'm not staying here.

IRMA: They want us to run, the Christians.

(*ASSAN enters.*)

ASSAN: Is it true what people are saying?

IRMA: What are they saying?

ASSAN: That the teacher is shooting people in the Square.

NADJA: There are bodies lying at the bus stop

On the pavement outside the electrical store.

Someone has fallen in the fountain

And turned the water there to muddy red.

IRMA: What are you going to do about it Assan?

ASSAN: What can I do?

(IRMA moves in on ASSAN to hint that she knows about his relationship with MARINA.)

IRMA: Maybe those extra lessons you took with the teacher
Those evenings sitting at his kitchen table.
Maybe they had their use after all.

ASSAN: What use?

IRMA: You know the layout of the house.
You could creep in,
Surprise him.
He's probably drunk anyway.

ASSAN: No.

IRMA: You're prepared to let him carry on shooting?

NADJA: They say the body in the fountain is the butcher's daughter.

ASSAN: Amela?

IRMA: She was your betrothed.
It's your duty to go.

ASSAN: I must tell him…

IRMA: What?

ASSAN: That Marina is alive.
(ASSAN starts to go.)

IRMA: Don't go without your gun.
*(ASSAN goes back into his house to fetch the gun.
Sound of wind.)*

NADJA: A hush has fallen on the town.

IRMA: People watch and wait behind closed doors.

NADJA / IRMA: The streets are empty
Even the dogs are hiding.
*(ASSAN crosses the stage with the gun.
HAMIDA enters and watches him.)*

IRMA: There's a pause for breath.

NADJA: No sign of life from the house in the square.

IRMA: But the next bloody bout will soon begin.
(ASSAN appears moving forward with the gun.)

NADJA / HAMIDA: Was that the sound of the back door opening?

IRMA: Shhh. It was the garden gate creaking in the wind.

NADJA: The man at the window takes a swig from his bottle.

HAMIDA: Trying to drown his grief and despair.

NADJA / IRMA: Was that the sound of an intruder in the kitchen?

IRMA: No. Just the cat jumping down from the chair.

NADJA: For a moment he rests his brow on the window pane.

HAMIDA: To cool the heat that rages inside.

NADJA / HAMIDA: Was that the sound of a foot on the stairway?

IRMA: No, it was nothing.

HAMIDA: Find somewhere to hide!

NADJA: When the figure of the boy appears in the doorway,

HAMIDA: Lover of his daughter, brother of his son,

NADJA: He's sitting on the bed, watching and waiting,

ASSAN: Sir, Marina's alive. Please give me the gun.

IRMA: Coldly and calmly the man raises the barrel,

HAMIDA: No.

NADJA: Intending to point towards his own head.

HAMIDA: Ahhh.

NADJA: The boy misinterprets,
Takes aim and fires

HAMIDA: No.
(*The wind dies.*)

IRMA: Blood

NADJA: On the counterpane.

IRMA / NADJA / HAMIDA: Borislav is dead.
(*ASSAN returns.*
Sound of birdsong.)

ASSAN: I thought he was going to kill me.

HAMIDA: What's done is done.

IRMA: And well done too.

ASSAN: He killed Sefat.

NADJA: All those bodies lying in the square.

ASSAN: I liked him.
I always liked him.

IRMA: Like is a weak word in a world of hate.
(*IRMA leaves.*
HAMIDA holds ASSAN and leads him off towards the house.
NADJA leaves.)

Scene 4

Sound of news in the background. MARINA enters. She has a piece of material and needle and thread. She measures out the ground where she intends burying BORISLAV. HAMIDA enters.

HAMIDA: I've brought you some coffee.
    (*MARINA doesn't answer.*)
    Marina.
    (*MARINA continues looking at the ground.*)
    You must keep up your strength.
    (*No response.*)
    He thought your father was going to shoot him.
    (*MARINA doesn't respond.*)
    He wanted to tell your father that you were safe.
    That's why he went there.
MARINA: I have to make his grave deep
    Otherwise the dogs will eat his body.
    A big black mongrel was eating one of the bodies in
    the square.
    I threw a stone at it
    And it ran off
    But I could see it on the other side of the fountain
    Waiting for me to leave.
    (*MARINA is sewing the material.*)
HAMIDA: He told me to leave you alone,
    He wants to come and comfort you
    But he's scared of causing you more pain.
MARINA: I thought I'd bury him here
    He liked sitting here
    Looking at the statue.
    He always said, 'I don't want a Christian burial!'
    Just as well
    The priest and the gravediggers have fled.
HAMIDA: It was not Assan's fault.
    It is Sefat you must blame.
MARINA: Sefat?
HAMIDA: Yes, Sefat.

MARINA: Sefat saved me.
  (*Pause.*
  The radio is turned off.)
HAMIDA: He saved you?
MARINA: They took me to the graveyard
  They held a knife to my throat
  One of them already had his trousers unbuttoned.
  Sefat stepped between them and me.
  'This is Rabbit.
  Don't you remember Rabbit?
  It'd be like doing it to your own sister.
  Go on, Rabbit,
  Let's see you run.'
  He made them laugh,
  That laughter saved my life.
  (*ASSAN is standing in the doorway.*)
HAMIDA: Don't tell me this.
MARINA: Why not?
  Would you prefer him to have killed me?
HAMIDA: I am Hamida,
  The woman who believed you should think the best
  of people.
  What sort of woman am I really
  Who was so ready to believe the worst of my son?
  Everything he did caused me pain,
  So I could never imagine him doing anything that would
  make me proud.
ASSAN: Mother.
HAMIDA: Don't call me that.
  I don't deserve the name.
  (*She goes.*)
MARINA: You thought he was going to shoot you. I know.
ASSAN: Yes.
MARINA: He thought I was dead.
ASSAN: When I told him you were alive
  It was too late.
MARINA: You mean he was already a murderer?
ASSAN: Yes.

MARINA: Who made him a murderer?
>   The man who wouldn't let me kill spiders in my bedroom?
>   He taught me how to trap them under a glass,
>   Slip a piece of paper underneath,
>   Carry them outside
>   And set them free in the garden.
>   (*Pause.*)
>   How old we've become
>   In just a few hours.
>   There was a girl who was planning to go to the capital
>   With her boyfriend.
>   Do you remember her?

ASSAN: I remember them both.

MARINA: They're dead.

ASSAN: Not us.

MARINA: Dead and buried
>   With all their dreams.

ASSAN: We could still escape.

MARINA: To where?
>   The capital?
>   The roads are blocked with tanks and mines.

ASSAN: We could find somewhere safe and wait.

MARINA: And then?

ASSAN: This cannot last forever.

MARINA: And then?
>   (*ASSAN doesn't respond.*)
>   Do you think I could lie with you now in the hay barn
>   And not smell his body rotting in the ground?
>   Do you think I could feel your fingers caress me
>   And not feel the hand that held the gun?
>   Do you think your whisper of love in the darkness
>   Could drown out my father's voice haunting my dreams?
>   Do you think I could ever look at our marriage bed
>   And not see blood on the counterpane?

ASSAN: If we loved each other…

MARINA: Your love will not hold out
>   When you look in my eyes and see no forgiveness.

And when you hold me in your arms and feel a heart of stone,
Will your grip be strong enough to make the blood flow again?
And when you kiss me and taste blame on my lips
Will your love make an antidote to the poison?
And will you never look at me and remember Sefat's death?

ASSAN: No.

MARINA: You'd try to hide it but you would feel it all the same.

ASSAN: I would never hide anything from you.
I love you.
Love is all we have.

MARINA: Then love the butcher's daughter,
It will be easier for you in the end.

ASSAN: Amela is…

MARINA: What?

(*She stops sewing.*)

ASSAN: Not for me.

(*Pause.*)

MARINA: She's dead.
I know.

(*Pause.*)

ASSAN: What will you do?

MARINA: Bury my father.
And then go to the hospital and help look after the dying.
There are not enough nurses.

ASSAN: But….

MARINA: What?
Do you think I don't belong there
Tending Muslim wounded?
I must pay my debt to your brother.

ASSAN: You can't stay here on your own.
Muslim fighters will try to defend the town
Christian guns will bombard it with shells.
They are threatening to blow up the dam.
Please come away with me.

MARINA: The Christian army is stronger
> They will take the town.
> Then I will become a Christian.
> A Christian who has never prayed to Jesus,
> A Christian who has never been to church,
> A Christian who has never read the Bible
> But a Christian is all I am allowed to be.
> And you must be a Muslim.
> Go and join their forces.
> I must make my father a shroud.
> (*There is sound of gunfire.*
> *She goes.*
> *Enter IRMA, HAMIDA and NADJA.*
> *They are carrying suitcases and bundles of belongings.*
> *The gunfire continues.*)

IRMA: Sabina?

HAMIDA: I'll go.
> (*She goes.*)

NADJA: The town is nearly surrounded.
> All the journalists and camera crews have left.

IRMA: Without you?

NADJA: He said it would be too dangerous.

IRMA: We have to stand and fight.
> This is just a temporary retreat.

NADJA: You were right about the horses and carts
> A pair of strong horses now will save your life.

IRMA / NADJA: A long trek before us
> In the cold and the rain.
> Down roads where a shell could drop at any moment
> Where a sniper's bullet could quite suddenly
> Find its mark.

NADJA: When they see those photos
> The rest of the world will be shocked into action.
> When they see what is happening to us
> On their TV screens.
> There will be such an outcry.
> Who could look at such things
> And not want to help?

They won't leave us here,
Trapped in a cage with madmen,
Scratching and fighting
To the death.
That would be barbaric.
They have to let us out.

IRMA: As long as there is breath in our bodies we will fight
We will reclaim what is ours
We will have vengeance
Even if it takes another hundred years.
(*Enter HAMIDA.*)

HAMIDA: Sabina refuses to leave her child's grave.
Are you ready Assan?

ASSAN: I'm not coming with you, Mother.

IRMA: He's a hero now.
He saved us from the teacher's bullets.
He killed his brother's murderer.
He avenged the death of his betrothed.
He must stay here and continue the fight.
One day a statue of your son may stand in this park.

HAMIDA: Please, Assan,
Come with us.

IRMA: There is no place for heroes on my cart.

ASSAN: Don't worry about me, Mother.

HAMIDA: I don't need to ride
I can walk.
Together we can walk.

ASSAN: It is a long way to safety.
Go with Irma.

IRMA: He knows where he belongs.
(*IRMA and NADJA hurry off.*
HAMIDA pauses and then goes too.
ASSAN stands and watches them.
MARINA drags her father's body onstage.
Sound of dogs snarling.
ASSAN goes. We think he has abandoned MARINA.
MARINA unfolds the shroud.

Suddenly ASSAN appears with a shovel.
She looks up at him.)

The End.

WISE GUYS

Characters

MIKE

His FATHER

His MOTHER

MARTIN, his brother

DARREN

SKID

POLICEMAN 1

WILL, Darren's grandfather

STEPHEN HURD

MAN IN THE STREET

POLICEMAN 2

POLICEMAN 3

Wise Guys was first performed on 30 October 1997 by Theatre Centre and Red Ladder Theatre Company, with the following cast:

STEPHEN / MARTIN, Michael Jempeji

SKID / WILL / MOTHER, Chand Martinez

MIKE, Justin Pierre

DARREN / DAD, Neil Thornton

Director, Antony McBride

Designer, Mary Robson

Composer, Ivan Stott

Choreographer, Lea Parkinson

Lighting Designer, Ace McCarron

ACT ONE

Home Sweet Home

FATHER: Fucking hell.

MIKE: So that bastard comes home drunk again. Front door slams. Falls over my brother Martin's bike in the hall doesn't he?

FATHER: How many times have I told you not to leave that bike there?

MIKE: And she gets up.

MOTHER: Keep your voice down. You'll wake the kids up.

FATHER: I'll wake that little sod up alright. He can come down here and shift this bike.

MIKE: I can hear him coming up the stairs. Freddy Krueger. Knocking the picture off the wall. Gave it to my Mum for her birthday. Can hear the glass splinter.

MOTHER: Dave, don't.

FATHER: Get your hands off me.

MIKE: I look over at Martin. He's just lying there. His eyes open. Got the look my hamster used to get when the cat came in the room.

FATHER: Martin!

MIKE: He's asleep.

FATHER: He can wake up.

MIKE: Leave him alone, Dad.

FATHER: He can come down here and shift this bike.

MIKE: Leave him.

FATHER: Martin!

MIKE: You're not going in there.

FATHER: Says who?

MIKE: Says me.

FATHER: Yeah?

MIKE: Yeah.

FATHER: Yeah?

MIKE: Yeah.

FATHER: You asking for a slap?

MIKE: No.

FATHER: No?

MIKE: No.

FATHER: Get out my way then.

(*MIKE doesn't move.*)

Think you're a man now, do you?

MIKE: And then his fist smashes into my face. And I'm on the floor and he's laying into me. And she's trying to stop him but he sends her flying along the landing and she bashes her head against the toilet door. He's got the end of the hoover and he's beating me over the head with it.

FATHER: Think you're hard, do you? I'll show you hard.

MIKE: And then it's over. He's out the door. And she's running after him trying to stop him. Stupid cow. She's running down the street and all the neighbours are watching. Blood dripping off her chin down her night-dress. What a sight. She wants him to stay. Couldn't give a toss about me.

MARTIN: Mike?

(*MARTIN goes to wipe MIKE's nose with a flannel.*)

MIKE: Get off.

MARTIN: You think it's broken?

MIKE: No.

(*MARTIN wipes MIKE's nose.*)

MARTIN: Can I sleep with you tonight?

MIKE: You wet the bed I'll kill you.

MARTIN: I won't.

MIKE: So we put the chest of drawers up against the door. Keep still. I wanna sleep.

MARTIN: You think he'll come back?

MIKE: I'll be ready for him.

MARTIN: I'm scared.

MIKE: If he tries to mash you he's a dead man.

MARTIN: Where's Mum?

MIKE: I don't know. Get to sleep.

MARTIN: Night, Mike.

MIKE: Shut up!

My brother Martin looks like one of those kids you see on TV at Christmas singing carols. Angelic. He's not. But he looks like it. I always felt like I had to protect him. 'Cos he was so much younger. I've been mean to him, don't get me wrong. Stole my Walkman and broke it one time. Closest I ever came to losing it with him. I mean I thumped him but not like to really hurt him. I'd never do that. At the end of the day he's the only person I care about. And I'm the only person he cares about. My Mum says I got too much influence over him. She's scared I'm going to lead him astray. I nearly got done for nicking car stereos and she's scared I'll get him into that. But I wouldn't. I'd kill him if he started that.

The Old Crowd

MIKE: There's three of us usually. Me.

DARREN: Darren.

SKID: Skid.

MIKE: His real name's Mark but when he was in Feltham he got called Skid for obvious reasons.

DARREN: Eh?

MIKE: Skidmark.

DARREN: Oh yeah.

MIKE: Darren's like a one megabyte computer. You gotta wait half an hour for the screen to change.

DARREN: Eh?

MIKE: Never mind.

DARREN: Oh yeah.

MIKE: Anyway like I was saying there's usually three of us. Skid smashes the window, I take the stereo out and Darren stands by with a rucksack and a bike to take it home. Like that. Very easy. Very safe. At the end of the day you don't get a lot each but there ain't much chance of getting caught. The person taking the stereo home has got the worst job 'cos mine takes two seconds, his takes, what? Ten minutes max.

DARREN: Who?

MIKE: What?

DARREN: Who's Max?

MIKE: Shut up, Darren.
Skid reckons I'm criminally minded. I walk down a street and I notice things that someone who weren't criminally minded wouldn't notice. Don't I, Skid?

SKID: Yeah.

MIKE: It's not nice. It's not normal. Like I see a laptop on a car seat or someone's wallet hanging out their back pocket. Or a door to a house left open. I notice them things.

DARREN: Or a car.

MIKE: What?

DARREN: Like a car you could rob.

MIKE: Yeah, well, Darren, it's quite likely you'd see a car if you're walking down the street.

SKID: Look.

MIKE: Right.

SKID: Where's your bike, Darren?

DARREN: Locked up to the railings.

SKID: You wanker.

DARREN: Didn't want anyone nicking it.

The Old Bill

MIKE: They picked Darren up at some traffic lights. The stupid git was sitting there waiting for the green outside the nick. I mean who ever heard of a cyclist waiting at traffic lights?

POLICEMAN 1: What you got in the bag, lad?

DARREN: Our cat.

POLICEMAN 1: Your cat?

DARREN: Yeah, I'm taking him to the vet.

POLICEMAN 1: Should get a cat box, lad.

DARREN: You can't carry a cat box on a bike.

POLICEMAN 1: That true?

DARREN: Yeah.

POLICEMAN 1: Never seen anyone carry a cat in a rucksack.

DARREN: He likes it.

POLICEMAN 1: Does he?

DARREN: Yeah.

POLICEMAN 1: Let's have a look, lad.

DARREN: You can't.

POLICEMAN 1: Why not?

DARREN: He doesn't like the light.

POLICEMAN 1: Why not?

DARREN: Hurts his eyes.

POLICEMAN 1: Open the bag.

DARREN: He'll jump out and scratch you.

POLICEMAN 1: I'm thick-skinned.

DARREN: He's got AIDS.

POLICEMAN 1: Your cat's got AIDS?

DARREN: Yeah, if he scratches you, you'll get it.

POLICEMAN 1: I'll take that risk, lad. Let's have a look.

MIKE: They know Darren hangs out with me but they can't prove nothing so I tell them to piss off. I got off that time. Darren got them so confused that they thought he was a head case and sent him to see a psychiatrist. The stupid git's proud of it. He goes round boasting that he's got a social worker.

DARREN: If it happens again my social worker reckons I'll get sent down.

MIKE: That true, Darren?

DARREN: Straight up. No word of a lie.

A Working Man

MIKE: Darren lives on the estate on the fifth floor with his Grandad. I hate going round there – it stinks. People who live there are like animals – they piss in the lift, they piss on the stairs and Darren's flat stinks of piss too – they got an incontinent dog. Least I think it's the dog – could be Darren's Grandad. Darren's Dad hasn't been around for years. And his Mum ran off with the bloke from the launderette where she worked. Flash git with a Merc. Darren went in there one day and found his Mum and this bloke pressed up against the dry cleaning machine in the back room. His Grandad's a pathetic case. Smoked so many fags all his life that his limbs are falling off one by one. Every time I go round there he's lost another arm or a leg. And he's dying of cancer. It's a miracle he's still alive.

WILL: Come in, Mike. Darren's just gone round to the offie to get me some baccy. Take a pew. You want a cup of tea?

MIKE: No thanks Mr McSherry. Just had me dinner.

I'm trying not to look at his new stump where the leg of his trousers is folded up and fastened with a safety pin.

WILL: You watching the match this afternoon?

MIKE: Which match is that, Mr McSherry?

WILL: The Scotland match of course.

MIKE: No. We're going to the park.

WILL: You're going to have your own game?

MIKE: Yeah.

WILL: They're a great team.

(*Sings quietly as MIKE speaks.*)

'Oh Flower of Scotland,

When will I see

Your like again' (*Etc.*)

MIKE: He's a boring git though. Came down here to work at Ford in Dagenham and drones on about the assembly lines and the picket lines and the fights he used to have with the management. Got made redundant in the end. When I look at old geezers like that it makes me want to spit. Anybody'd think that screwing a bolt on a chassis was the most interesting job in the world.

WILL: I used to take home a hundred and fifty quid a week.

MIKE: That true, Mr McSherry?

WILL: That was a lot in those days.

MIKE: Yeah, Mr McSherry.

WILL: You could hold your head up because you were earning your living and looking after your family. You could take pride in it. Not like now.

MIKE: No, Mr McSherry.

WILL: There's only work for women nowadays. Computer bloody programmers.

MIKE: That's right, Mr McSherry.

I'm starting to feel a bit sick what with the smell of piss and the stink of cabbage and old man McSherry waving his stump around.

WILL: You should see the car I had as well. But ye could afford to run it, ye see.

MIKE: Yeah.

WILL: Ah, there's Darren.

DARREN: Alright then, Mike?

MIKE: Alright, Darren.

WILL: Just wheel me to the toilet before ye go, pal.

MIKE: They're in there ages. Hate to think what Darren's having to do for him. I mean I know it's tragic and all that but you wouldn't catch me wiping nobody's arse. Not if you paid me a million pounds. Darren never even looks put out about it.

WILL: Go on then laddie. Are you not taking a ball?

DARREN: Eh?

MIKE: Skid's bringing a ball.

WILL: Skid? Is he that one who was in borstal?

MIKE: Feltham, Mr McSherry.

WILL: Well, make sure you're back before midnight, Darren.

MIKE: So we leave him puffing away in front of the rugby.

WILL: Look after him, Mike.

MIKE: I will. I hate going round Darren's.

A Chance Encounter

DARREN: Yo, Skid! Where's the ball?

SKID: What ball?

DARREN: Mike said we was going to play football.

MIKE: No, Darren. I couldn't tell your Grandad we was meeting Skid cause he's been to see his fence, could I?

DARREN: Oh.

SKID: There you are, thirty for you. Ten for Darren.

DARREN: Why do I only get a tenner?

MIKE: 'Cos me and Skid are the brains.

SKID: You just do the leg work.

DARREN: I'm saving.

SKID: What for?

DARREN: Take my Grandad on holiday.

MIKE: Where to?

DARREN: Scotland.

SKID: Wouldn't mind going there some time. I got contacts in Glasgow.

DARREN: He wants to show me the Highlands where his family's from.

SKID: You'd look good in a kilt, Daz.

MIKE: You want to be a flower of Scotland, Darren?

SKID: Pansy of Scotland.

DARREN: Shut up.

SKID: I'm going to get absofuckinlutely wrecked tonight. I'm going to see that geezer.

MIKE: Oh yeah.

SKID: You want some?

MIKE: Couple.

SKID: Right.

DARREN: What geezer?

SKID: Mind your own business, Darren.

DARREN: No, but what are you going to see him about?

SKID: A dog.

DARREN: You gettin' a dog?

MIKE: No, Darren, he's getting some sweeties.

DARREN: (*Trying to tackle MIKE.*) You what?

MIKE: Some pills, you div.

SKID: You want some Darren?

DARREN: I don't know.

SKID: Oh, I forgot, you don't. Your Grandad won't let you!

MIKE: Leave him!

SKID: Rich pickings round here mate. Tossers with a lot of money like living near a park.

(*Someone whistles.*)

DARREN: Awwwh look at that dog. I love Dalmatians.

SKID: You're soft Dazzer.

DARREN: Mike.

MIKE: What?

DARREN: Look who it is.

MIKE: Who?

DARREN: With the dog. Just come out of that house.

MIKE: Who is it?

DARREN: Stephen Hurd.

MIKE: Hurd the nerd?

SKID: Who's Stephen Hurd?

MIKE: Wanker from our school.

DARREN: Mike put a dog turd in his locker one time.

MIKE: Just a bit of fun.

DARREN: Remember? He just disappeared one week. Never came back.

MIKE: I heard he was in a loony bin. Here, Hurdy.

STEPHEN: Oh hi.

MIKE: Alright?

STEPHEN: Yeah. You?

MIKE: Yes thanks. Your dog?

STEPHEN: No, I'm looking after it for some friends.

MIKE: You live here?

STEPHEN: No. I'm house-sitting for them for a few weeks. Here, boy.

MIKE: Wow. Big house.

STEPHEN: Yes.

MIKE: Very nice. Overlooking the park.

SKID: That their Range Rover in the drive?

STEPHEN: Yes.

MIKE: Cool. So you're living here while they're away.

STEPHEN: Yes.

DARREN: Cor, you got this whole house to yourself?

STEPHEN: Well, there's the dog as well.

SKID: He looks like he could give you a nasty lick.

STEPHEN: He's quite fierce. Well, I'd better take him for his walk.

MIKE: So where's the owners?

STEPHEN: Away.

MIKE: Oh yeah. Where?

STEPHEN: Umm. In Italy.

MIKE: How do you know them?

STEPHEN: One of them's my lecturer from college.

DARREN: Your what?

MIKE: His lecturer, Darren. That means his teacher. So like they've left you in charge of their house and their dog and their Range Rover.

STEPHEN: Well –

MIKE: They must really trust you.

STEPHEN: I think they're coming back soon.

SKID: Thought you said they was away for a few weeks.

STEPHEN: Oh yeah but –

MIKE: So, you're going to college.

STEPHEN: Yeah.

MIKE: What you studying?

STEPHEN: Photography.

MIKE: Cool. You going to be like a journalist?

STEPHEN: I don't know.

MIKE: I wouldn't mind being a photographer.

STEPHEN: Right.

SKID: I wouldn't mind taking pictures for *Penthouse*. You ever done that?

STEPHEN: No.

MIKE: Well, it's good to see you anyway, Hurdy.

STEPHEN: Yeah, well, I better go.

MIKE: Alright. Bye then.

STEPHEN: Bye.

MIKE: Nice to see you're doing so well, mate.

STEPHEN: Yeah and you.

MIKE: You what?

STEPHEN: What?

MIKE: Nothing.

(*STEPHEN goes.*)

DARREN: Pussy.

SKID: Bet there's some stuff in there worth nicking.

DARREN: Yeah.

An Evening with The Waltons

MIKE: So there we are: Me, Martin, our Mum and Freddy
Krueger. He's in one of his rare good moods which means
it's early in the evening before he's had too many cans. I
hate it when he's in a good mood. Sits there on the sofa
with his arm round her and she snuggles up to him. He's
got his vest on and there's all this hair sprouting out all
over from his chest and his armpits and his nose and his
lug-holes. And she's got her fingers in it stroking him.
Reminds me of the chimpanzee house at the Zoo.
And he's got Martin bouncing up and down on his knee.
Flying into the air and then coming down and bouncing up
again. And Martin's giggling like we're a real family and
Freddy's a real Dad. God! He used to do that with me.

FATHER: Alright, Mike?

MIKE: Yeah.

FATHER: Want a beer?

MIKE: No thanks.

FATHER: Come on.

MOTHER: Don't you want a beer, Mike?

MIKE: What are we, the Waltons all of a sudden? Next thing
you know we'll be saying, 'Good night John boy', before
we go to sleep.

FATHER: Need a shave lad.

MIKE: You need your coat clipping mate, but I don't go on
about it.

FATHER: Look at you. Could grow a beard.
(*He rubs MIKE's chin.*)
Right little man.
(*He puts his arm around MIKE's neck.*)
That's a headlock, lad. Get out of that.

MIKE: I hate this. I hate it! It's like it used to be. When I was
five, six. Times like this I used to think everything was
gonna change. And we really were going to go and live
in the little house on the prairie or wherever it is that the
Waltons do all their John boy crap. I used to think if I tried
hard enough things would stay like this. But then come
midnight he'd be hitting me over the head with his belt

179

again and we'd be back on Elm Street.

So anyway there I am with my head in his smelly armpit when…

(*Doorbell.*)

MOTHER: Go and see who that is, Mart.

MARTIN: No.

(*MOTHER goes.*)

MIKE: What's wrong with you?

MARTIN: Nothing.

MIKE: You got your frightened hamster look on you.

(*MOTHER returns.*)

FATHER: Who is it?

MOTHER: The police.

FATHER: What's he done now?

MIKE: But it isn't me they want to talk to. It's Martin. And shit hits the fan.

MARTIN: It weren't me. It was Brendan.

MOTHER: The shopkeeper told the police it was both of you.

MARTIN: We only took some CDs.

MOTHER: And a Walkman.

MARTIN: Brendan took that.

MOTHER: And you stood at the counter and knocked over a display.

MARTIN: It was a crap Walkman. Weren't worth nicking.

(*MIKE laughs.*

MARTIN takes this as a cue to laugh himself.)

We should have gone for the video camera.

FATHER: You're just like your bloody brother. Come here.

MIKE: And he's unbuckling his belt and pulling it through the loops.

MARTIN: It was Brendan's idea.

MIKE: And the strap's singing as it slashes through the air. And Martin's running round the room trying to find shelter. Looking for something solid to put between him and the belt. Something bigger and stronger to take the rap. Like big brother for instance. He's cowering behind me and the strap's whistling round my ears.

Leave him alone.

FATHER: Get out the way.

MIKE: Listen to his side of the story, can't you?

FATHER: If it wasn't for you he wouldn't be going out thieving.

MIKE: What you mean? Ain't my fault. Got a brilliant role-model in you, innit?

MOTHER: Don't you start, Mike.

MIKE: You never stole anything in your life, did ya?

MOTHER: It's you that he's copying.

MIKE: Where did the telly come from, then?

MOTHER: That's got nothing to do with anything.

MIKE: You always take that bastard's side. Look at him. Fucking pyscho.

FATHER: I told you to get out of my way.

MIKE: If you lay one hand on Martin I'll deck you. And just as he's lifting the belt for another go at me I catch sight of the table lamp. It's a woman standing holding the light bulb up in her hand and she's standing on this great big bit of metal – what do they call it? A plinth. Looks pretty useful at this particular moment. So out goes my arm and just as I feel the belt whistle past my ears I bring it down on his head. And everything goes quiet. I'm left standing with the lady of the lamp dripping blood in my hand.

MOTHER: You stupid sod. What have you done?

MIKE: Killed him I hope.

MOTHER: Get out!

MIKE: What?

MOTHER: Get out! Go on.

MIKE: Why?

MOTHER: I don't want you here, Mike. I can't take it any more. Just go!

MIKE: I can feel my insides starting to shudder and some bastard's dropped an Alka Seltzer tablet in me eyes.

MOTHER: Go on.

(*He looks at MARTIN.*)

MIKE: Sod you then.

(*He goes.*)

Goodfellas

MIKE: Skid got himself chucked out of home when he was fourteen. He was put in a children's home but as soon as he could he got a flat with some bit of skirt he was knocking around with. While Skid was in Feltham she moved some other geezer in. He soon had them sorted though. You don't double-cross Skid and get away with it. He's watching a video when I get round there. *Goodfellas*. The air's blue with the smoke of several hour's worth of green. Darren's there too sprawled out in a smelly armchair that came with the flat. Skid's got a big collection of all them old films. Used to have them on VHS but now he's upgraded to DVD. Spends all his time watching them over and over. *Goodfellas* is one of his favourites. He's seen it twenty-eight times: twelve times at the cinema and another fifteen times on video.

SKID: Sixteen.

MIKE: I've watched it four times with him but I prefer the old horror movies meself. *Goodfellas* is the one with Ray Liotta and Robert de Niro.

SKID: And Joe Pesci.

DARREN: Which one's Joe Pesci?

SKID: Him!

MIKE: Skid's favourite scene is the one where Joe Pesci shoots the waiter in the bar.

SKID: Spider.

DARREN: Where?

SKID: That's the name of the kid. The waiter.

MIKE: He shot this kid, this waiter, in the foot and the next time he sees him Joe Pesci tells the kid to do a dance for him and the kid tells him where to get off.

(*SKID quotes Spider's line from the film.*)

And de Niro asks Joe Pesci if he's gonna let the kid, Spider, get away with it.

SKID: He's trying to make a joke of it.

MIKE: But Joe Pesci's a complete psycho and he doesn't like anybody taking the piss. So he just takes out his gun and shoots the kid. Well Skid thinks this is the most brilliant scene ever written by anybody in the whole history of time.

SKID: It's true.

DARREN: Better than *Spiderman*?

(*The other two look at him in disgust.*)

MIKE: He even found it printed in some film magazine and spent half his dole cheque photocopying it and sending it out to his friends. And he'd got one of them fluorescent felt tips and gone over the best lines with it.

MIKE: Skid?

SKID: Shhh. Look at Joe Pesci. (*He quotes Tommy's line from the film.*)

MIKE: Skid?

SKID: What? (*He repeats Spider's line from the film.*)

MIKE: Can I doss here for a bit?

(*SKID quotes Jimmy's line from the film.*)

Can I?

SKID: Eh?

MIKE: Stay here.

SKID: Sure. Look, watch! Ahhh, Yeah.

MIKE: What you looking at?

DARREN: Nothing.

MIKE: Skid's hitting the bookmark button and the scene's starting again and Ray Liotta's shouting and laughing and Spider's limping up to the table with his foot in plaster and Joe Pesci's having a go at the kid all over again.

(*MIKE and SKID repeat Tommy's line from the film.*)

DARREN: You gonna live here?

MIKE: Duh, dat's what dossing usually means, Darren.

DARREN: Why?

MIKE: 'Cos I got nowhere else to live dumbo.

DARREN: Why?

MIKE: 'Cos I got chucked out of home.

DARREN: Why?

MIKE: Shut up, Darren.

DARREN: What happened though?

MIKE: Mind your own business. God!

SKID: Shut up both of you. Show some respect. Now, watch.
(*Music into the club.*)

Ecstasy

DARREN: I'm buzzing. I'm really buzzing.

SKID: We all are, Darren.

DARREN: I know, but it's like, shit. Like the world's a really
beautiful place, you know what I mean?

MIKE: Yeah, we know what you mean.

DARREN: And like everyone's really friendly and shit. I
mean really friendly.

SKID: Yeah.

DARREN: I mean like they've got love coming out of their
eyes. They smile at ya and ya just wanna go over and give
them a hug.

MIKE: Stop laughing, Skid. He's serious, man.

DARREN: I am. I love you two, you know.

SKID: You turning gay, Daz?

DARREN: We been through some real shit together, ain't we?
I reckon I know you two better than what I know anyone
else in the whole world. I feel like I could trust you with
my life, man.

SKID: It's the drug, Darren, it's not real.

MIKE: Maybe this is real.

SKID: Eh?

MIKE: Maybe this is how things are meant to be.

DARREN: Yeah, that's right.

MIKE: I mean this is how it should be. We should feel like
this all the time. And the rest of the time when we don't
feel like this is the time that's not real.

DARREN: I mean, Mike, you'd never let me down, would ya?

MIKE: 'Course I wouldn't.

DARREN: I wouldn't let you down. I'd do anything for you,
man.

SKID: Look here, lover boys, you can spend the evening
slobbering over each other if you want. I'm interested in
some proper action. See her? She's coming home with me.

MIKE: You're all mouth, Skid.

SKID: Just 'cos you never pull, mate.

MIKE: What?

SKID: You don't, do you? Or if you do they always end up
chucking you. You just haven't got the touch Mike. Now
watch and learn.

(*SKID goes.*)

DARREN: The music really gets to ya, don't it?

MIKE: Yeah.

Then I saw this girl. She's got that sort of hair that you get
in them poxy shampoo ads. Every time she turns round
it sort of flies out except it don't look poxy to me in my
present frame of mind. It looks sort of real. And it's like it
really is slow motion.

(*DARREN dances.*)

MIKE: Get off, Darren.

DARREN: What?

MIKE: Get off.

So I start chatting her up.

DARREN: Mike.

MIKE: Go away, Darren.

Letting her know that I'm flush and that I might not have
got me money totally legally.

DARREN: Mike, I think…

MIKE: I told you to leave me alone.

And just as I'm moving in for the kill Stephen Hurd turns
up. And he's got two pints of lager in his hands. She takes
hers and goes and talks to her friend.

MIKE: Hello, Hurdy.

DARREN: She your girlfriend, Hurdy?

STEPHEN: Sort of.

DARREN: Saw you dancing with her.

STEPHEN: Right.

DARREN: Mike was trying to chat her up.

STEPHEN: Well, I'll see you around.

DARREN: Yeah see ya.

MIKE: See ya.

(*STEPHEN goes.*)

DARREN: Want a dance, Mike?

MIKE: Piss off, Darren.

   (*SKID returns.*)

SKID: We're going back to hers.

DARREN: Wow.

SKID: Never mind, Mike, Darren will let you stick it in
   tonight.

   (*SKID, DARREN and STEPHEN all dance in different places
   on the dance floor. DARREN and SKID are enjoying themselves.
   They try to get MIKE to join in. It is clear that he is trying to block
   out his feelings of rejection. He's a little too manic maybe. Every
   time there is contact between him and STEPHEN, STEPHEN
   feels very threatened.*)

The Hangover

MIKE and DARREN are watching The Waltons.

DARREN: I couldn't sleep, man.

   (*MIKE doesn't respond.*)

   Great night though.

   (*No response.*)

   My Grandad asked me what was wrong with me eyes.

MIKE: Not surprised. State you were in.

DARREN: Skid still not back?

MIKE: No.

DARREN: Skid always pulls, don't he?

   (*MIKE doesn't respond.*)

   Fancy Stephen Hurd having a bird like that.

MIKE: She was a slag.

DARREN: Yeah.

   (*MIKE is drinking from a can of lager.*)

   What shall we do tonight?

MIKE: I don't know.

DARREN: I feel like getting absofuckinlutely wrecked.

MIKE: You haven't got anything to get wrecked on.

   (*DARREN says nothing.*)

   Have you?

DARREN: Maybe.

MIKE: What?

(*DARREN doesn't respond.*)

What you got?

DARREN: Some heroin.

MIKE: You what? Where you get heroin?

DARREN: It's pure.

MIKE: You're full of shit, Darren.

(*DARREN holds up a phial.*)

Where you get that?

DARREN: You want some?

MIKE: Your Grandad's morphine, isn't it?

DARREN: No.

MIKE: How you get that? Rob it from that nurse, did ya?

DARREN: No.

MIKE: You sad bastard.

DARREN: Shut up.

MIKE: Your poor Grandad has to have a MacMillan nurse and all you can do is tief his morphine off her.

DARREN: I'm not tiefing. Just shut up, okay?

MIKE: Darren's tiefing off his Grandad.

(*He splashes him with lager.*)

DARREN: (*Almost in tears.*) Get off. Get off.

MIKE: Oooh, he's going to cry.

(*MIKE starts hitting DARREN.*
The door bell goes.)

Go and see who that is.

(*DARREN goes.*
MIKE flicks through the channels on the TV.
DARREN returns with MARTIN.)

Martin!

MARTIN: Hi.

MIKE: Long time no see. New trainers?

MARTIN: Yeah, Mum bought 'em me.

MIKE: Haven't missed your birthday, have I?

MARTIN: My others were crap. I couldn't show myself in them no more.

MIKE: So why ain't you been round?

MARTIN: Been playing on my computer.

MIKE: What computer?

MARTIN: Dad got it.

MIKE: Off the back of a lorry?

MARTIN: It's got DVD and a video camera. I got it set up in the bedroom.

MIKE: Where?

MARTIN: I got a desk now.

MIKE: There's no room for a desk.

MARTIN: There is.

MIKE: Where?

MARTIN: Where your bed was.

MIKE: You what?

MARTIN: What?

MIKE: They got rid of my bed?

MARTIN: You don't need it. Can I have a lager?

MIKE: No, you bloody can't.

MARTIN: Piss off.

MIKE: What? You swearing at me? Don't you swear at me.

MARTIN: Bugger off.

(*DARREN laughs.*)

MIKE: Shut up, Darren.

MARTIN: Arsehole.

(*DARREN and MARTIN both laugh.*)

MIKE: Martin just stop that.

DARREN: He's pissed off today, Martin.

MARTIN: Why?

DARREN: 'Cause this girl didn't fancy him last night.

MARTIN: Does he fancy her?

DARREN: Yeah.

MARTIN: You'll have to have a wank instead, Mike.

(*DARREN laughs.*)

MIKE: I told you to shut it.

MARTIN: You gonna make me?

MIKE: Yeah, if you're not careful.

MARTIN: Oooh, oooh.

MIKE: Just shut it.

MARTIN: Ooh, Mike, do it again.

MIKE: I'm warning you.

(*MARTIN makes orgasm noises.*)

Stop it.

MARTIN: That's what you sound like. When you wank.

(*He makes more orgasm noises.*)

He used to think I was asleep. Nobody could sleep through that racket.

(*He makes more noises.*

Suddenly MIKE starts hitting him furiously.)

DARREN: Mike!

(*MIKE continues.*)

Mike, stop it.

MIKE: Little bastard.

DARREN: Stop it, man.

(*MIKE is still trying to hit MARTIN.*

DARREN restrains him.)

He's your brother man.

(*MIKE stops.*

MARTIN is lying curled up. He is sobbing.

On the TV the Waltons are being nice to each other.

MIKE stares at the screen.

MARTIN is still sobbing.)

MIKE: (*To the TV.*) Shut up!

(*He uses the remote to switch off the TV.*)

Morphine

MIKE: I don't care what people think of me. You gotta look out for number one cos nobody else ain't going to. If someone stands in my way I'm going to have 'em.

DARREN: Is it affecting you?

MIKE: Yeah.

DARREN: Yeah.

MIKE: Everybody's on the take at the end of the day. Only thing is that some of us are called crims for doing it and others are called, what's the word? Entrepreneurs.

DARREN: Entrep…

MIKE: If you're posh you get a knighthood for robbing people.

DARREN: On trip…

MIKE: And if you're like me then you're likely to end up in the nick.

DARREN: On trippers.

MIKE: I mean how much is a new car? How much is it to tax and insure it? How am I going to earn that sort of money?

DARREN: How much is an Audi TT?

MIKE: Twenty thousand.

DARREN: Shit.

MIKE: I ain't going and slaving my guts away like Darren's Dad. Grandad. Nice set of wheels he's got, innit?

DARREN: What would you have?

MIKE: What?

DARREN: If you could have any car?

MIKE: Don't know.

DARREN: Skid's going to get an Aston Martin.

MIKE: Yeah?

DARREN: He knows how to get things Skid.

MIKE: Mmmm.

DARREN: Just goes and gets them.

MIKE: Anything Skid can get. I can get.

DARREN: (*Placatory.*) Oh yeah.

MIKE: So after the morphine wore off we took some wiz and we went out on our own to indulge in a bit of private enterprise.

Private Enterprise

DARREN: That one, Mike.

MIKE: Alright, Darren.

DARREN: Wait, wait.

MIKE: What?

DARREN: What's this guy doing?

MIKE: Where?

DARREN: Over there by the bus stop.

MIKE: Waiting for a bus.

DARREN: Yeah, but he's looking, man.

MIKE: Well stop acting so suspicious and then he won't look.

DARREN: Yeah, but why's he looking at me, man?

MIKE: Because your eyes are popping out of your head and you keep whispering in my ear.

DARREN: Yeah, but Mike, man –

MIKE: Shut up, Darren.

DARREN: You going to do it?

MIKE: Yeah.

DARREN: He can see us.

MIKE: Not from that distance. So the Toyota, yeah?

DARREN: Yeah. Mike!

MIKE: What?

DARREN: He's using his mobile phone.

MIKE: So?

DARREN: He's probably phoning the police.

MIKE: He's probably phoning his wife to say he's going to be late home.

DARREN: He is Mike, he's phoning the police. I wish Skid was here.

MIKE: Who you phoning, mate?

MAN: Pardon?

MIKE: Who you phoning?

MAN: Mind your own business.

MIKE: Who you phoning?

MAN: I'm not telling you.

(*DARREN grabs the phone.*)

Give it back.

DARREN: Mike. Get him off me, Mike.

(*MIKE hits the man over the head.*
He collapses.)

MIKE: Come on, Darren.

So we smashed the window of a nice red Toyota and got in. Trouble was the wanker did get through to the filth. This unmarked car started chasing us.

DARREN: It's the cops.

The Chase

DARREN: They got a video in there, man. They're videoing us. They got a video in the car, Mike. Awhh shit. They got me on video.

MIKE: Don't show your face then.

DARREN: And they got my picture on computer. What you going to do Mike?

MIKE: Just watch.

So I drove as near as I could to the car in front. Shoved the Toyota in reverse and…

POLICEMAN 2: They're going to ram us. Watch out.

MIKE: …smacked into the front of the unmarked car. Then I pulled out into the oncoming traffic and drove at it. They all got out the way quick enough.

DARREN: They're following us, Mike. My Grandad'll kill me.

MIKE: What with? His stump?

DARREN: They're getting closer. We're going to get sent down. We shouldn't have done it without Skid.

MIKE: Shut up, Darren.

We're heading along Old Ford Road now and I take a quick left with the Jacks burning rubber behind me.

DARREN: (*Looking at a wall in front of them.*) Mike!

MIKE: We come to a dead end. So we legged it over the wall, found ourselves in a churchyard.

DARREN: They gone?

MIKE: Shhhh!

(*They listen.*)

DARREN: What we gonna do now?

MIKE: We can't go home empty-handed.

DARREN: You must be joking.

MIKE: Found a nice little Peugeot parked in front of the vicarage. And we were off again. This time no cops.

(*MIKE and DARREN are in a much more cramped car. The police appear behind them.*)

POLICEMAN 3: It's the same ones.

POLICEMAN 2: Keep well back. Don't let them see us.

(*DARREN keeps looking behind.*)

MIKE: Chill out, Darren.

So we drove back to the flat feeling pretty pleased with the night's activities. Home sweet home.

Come on Darren.

(*They get out of the car.*)

POLICEMAN 3: Gotcha.

POLICEMAN 2: Let them get into the flat first.

The Great Escape

MIKE: Skid was home when we got back. So we gave him the low-down.

And then we rammed the bastards.

DARREN: We had to leg it.

SKID: So you've dumped it?

DARREN: Yeah but we got another one.

SKID: What, another car?

MIKE: 'Course.

SKID: Where is it?

MIKE: In the car park.

SKID: You what?

MIKE: What?

SKID: You brought it back here?

MIKE: We'd shaken the shit off by that time.

That's when there was a knock on the door.

SKID: You wankers.

MIKE: And all hell lets loose. Skid runs into the bog and grabs a bag of pills.

DARREN: What'll my Grandad do if I get sent down? I was going to take him to Scotland.

MIKE: Give me strength.

DARREN: He was going to show me Loch Lomond, take me to Skye.

MIKE: I'll put you in the sky if you don't shut up. You'll be up there playing a harp.

POLICEMAN 2: Police. Open up!

MIKE: Skid's in the front room now and he's opened the door to the balcony.

SKID: Come on. We'll have to jump down.

MIKE: And the Dibble's banging the door down. So we go out on the balcony.

DARREN: I'm scared of heights.

MIKE: And the wood in the door frame is beginning to crack. Darren!

SKID: Leave him if he won't come.

MIKE: Come on, you wanker jump.

And door's beginning to give way.

I'll take you to Scotland.

DARREN: Promise?

MIKE: Promise.

And Darren jumps off the balcony just as the nippleheads break into the flat.

SKID: You wankers. They'll turn that flat upside down.

DARREN: It was Mike's idea.

SKID: Didn't have time to get me gear. Only got the pills.

DARREN: What we gonna do?

SKID: Well we can't go back to the flat thanks to you two dickheads.

DARREN: They might go looking for me at me Grandad's.

SKID: Shut up! I'm thinking.

The Hideout

MIKE: Sorry to bother you and all that.

STEPHEN: It's okay.

(*Dog barks.*)

Quiet, Luciano.

MIKE: You what?

STEPHEN: That what he's called.

SKID: Nice place.

MIKE: You're a long way from home.

DARREN: No, he's not. He was brought up in Clapton. Look at this, man.

STEPHEN: Careful.

DARREN: What?

STEPHEN: Nothing.

SKID: Your mate's scared clumsy great oafs like us is going to come in here breaking things, Mike.

STEPHEN: No.

MIKE: Lot of books.

STEPHEN: Yes.

MIKE: They read them all?

STEPHEN: I don't know.

SKID: (*Picking up STEPHEN's camera.*) Nice camera.

STEPHEN: Yeah.

SKID: You got anything to drink then?

STEPHEN: Oh yeah, sure.

(*He goes.*)

SKID: Hey, Darren.

(*He pretends to piss into the vase.*
They laugh.)

That Range Rover.

MIKE: What?

SKID: Useful car.

DARREN: We could go to Scotland in it.

MIKE: Don't be daft, Darren.

DARREN: You promised.

MIKE: You're obsessed.

DARREN: We could take a tent.

MIKE: I'm not going to Scotland in a tent.

SKID: I fancy a trip to Glasgow. See my mate. Do some business.

MIKE: He'd be on to the Feds in no time.

SKID: He's scared, Darren.

MIKE: No, I'm not.

SKID: So get it off him.

MIKE: I don't know.

SKID: I'll get it off him.

MIKE: Skid!

SKID: What?

MIKE: I'll do it.

(*STEPHEN returns with the lager.*)

STEPHEN: Lager.

MIKE: Great.

DARREN: Thanks mate.

MIKE: So that car out there.

STEPHEN: Yeah?

MIKE: They let you drive it?

STEPHEN: Haven't passed me test yet.

(*SKID and DARREN laugh.*)

MIKE: You could go anywhere.

STEPHEN: Gotta look after the house and the dog.

DARREN: You let us borrow it?

MIKE: Darren's Grandad's from Scotland, see, and he's dying of cancer and we thought we'd take him there.

STEPHEN: Right.

MIKE: But we ain't got a car, see.

STEPHEN: Yes,

MIKE: So we thought maybe you'd lend us the Range Rover.

STEPHEN: You wouldn't be insured.

SKID: Scared we might scratch the paintwork?

(*DARREN laughs. SKID signs to MIKE to get on with it.*)

MIKE: You saying you wouldn't help a dying man?

STEPHEN: No.

MIKE: What 'No, you're not saying that' or 'No, you won't help a dying man'?

STEPHEN: It's not my car.

SKID: Oooh, sorry. You mustn't drive a car without the owner's consent, Mike. Where are the keys?

STEPHEN: I can't remember.

SKID: He can't remember. Mind you don't break anything, Darren.

DARREN: Eh?

SKID: I mean it would be a pity if you went over there and knocked that vase over wouldn't it?

DARREN: Would it?

SKID: Or you might smash that camera.

STEPHEN: They're in the kitchen.

SKID: Where?

STEPHEN: In a cupboard.

SKID: Which cupboard?

STEPHEN: Over the sink.

(*SKID nods to DARREN who goes.*)

SKID: He thinks you're a dangerous driver, Mike. You don't appreciate people casting doubt on your driving skills, do you?

MIKE: No.

(*DARREN returns.*)

SKID: What you eating?

DARREN: Dunno. What is it?

STEPHEN: Smoked salmon.

SKID: You naughty boy. You didn't ask. Give him the keys, Darren.

DARREN: Why?

SKID: They're not yours. They're his.

(*DARREN gives STEPHEN the keys.*)

SKID: So?

STEPHEN: What?

SKID: You going to let your mate, Mike, have the keys?

(*STEPHEN and MIKE look at each other.*)

Don't you trust him? Eh?

STEPHEN: I don't know.

DARREN: They got a tent?

STEPHEN: Who?

DARREN: The people who own this place.

STEPHEN: I don't know.

SKID: Look in the garage, Darren.

(*DARREN goes again.*)

You wanna phone the police? You can borrow my mobile.

(*He holds out his phone.*)

We don't want to force him to do anything he don't want to do, do we Mike?

MIKE: No.

SKID: Phone them. Here. (*He pretends to dial 999. Holding the phone out to STEPHEN.*) It's ringing.

STEPHEN: I don't want to.

SKID: So you're going to let him have the keys?

(*STEPHEN and MIKE look at each other.*)

SKID: They wanna know which service.

STEPHEN: Mike, I can't.

MIKE: Give me the keys then.

(*SKID holds out the phone, STEPHEN gives MIKE the keys.*)

SKID: Sorry, wrong number.

(*DARREN returns.*)

DARREN: I think I found a tent.

SKID: Come on then.

(*MIKE and DARREN start to go.*
SKID stops them.)

Don't you want to come with us, mate?

STEPHEN: No I…

MIKE: Skid, come on. Leave him.

SKID: Thought you were a photographer. Lots of photo opportunities in Scotland.

STEPHEN: I gotta look after the house.

SKID: I think you oughta come and look after the car.

STEPHEN: What about the dog?

SKID: What about him?

STEPHEN: I can't leave him.

DARREN: He can come with us. Be company for Scot.

SKID: Yeah! Come on.

End of Act One.

ACT TWO

On the High Road

MIKE: Never been to Scotland. Never been anywhere up North. Never wanted to. Freddy Krueger was going to take us to Alton Towers one time. Got lost, ended up in Wolverhampton. Didn't get lost this time though. Found Glasgow alright. No thanks to Darren. Dropped Skid in Sauciehall Street in the middle of the night.

DARREN: I wish he was coming with us.

WILL: He should be careful. It can be a rough place.

MIKE: Yeah?

WILL: People with knives. All sorts.

(*He winces in pain.*)

DARREN: You alright, Grandad?

WILL: Give me some of that.

(*DARREN gives him some medicine.*)

MIKE: I hate the fuckin countryside. Nothing but rich bastards in the countryside. And cows and sheep pissing and shitting everywhere. And wankers in Range Rovers with dogs jumping round in the back. Which way here Darren?

DARREN: Uhhh….

MIKE: Left?

DARREN: Yeah?

MIKE: I can't see out the mirror with those dogs sticking their heads up!

DARREN: Get down Scot.

MIKE: M8 West?

DARREN: Yeah.

MIKE: Right.

(*They veer left.*)

DARREN: I mean, no. No! Right!

(*They veer right.*)

MIKE: 'Kin 'ell! Let him read the map!

DARREN: Who?

MIKE: Stephen. Least he's got half a brain.

DARREN: I'm the navigator.

MIKE: Get that dog down!

STEPHEN: Sit Luciano.

WILL: (*Woozily.*) It's a queer name that.

(*The boys laugh.*
WILL sings 'Nessun Dorma'.)

DARREN: Will we see Loch Lomond, Mike?

MIKE: How the fuck do I know?

WILL: It's a great car, Stephen.

STEPHEN: Thanks.

WILL: Very kind of your friends to lend it to us.

DARREN: Will we see Loch Lomond, Grandad?

WILL: You're a very quiet laddie, Stephen. Isn't he, Mike, he's very quiet your pal.

MIKE: Yeah.

WILL: Very quiet. Very nice car. Very good of you all to do this. I wasna sure about you. But you're a good lad. You're all good lads.

DARREN: Grandad!

WILL: Aye, laddie?

DARREN: Will we see Loch Lomond?

MIKE: For fuck's sake, Darren!

DARREN: What?

MIKE: Shut up about Loch Lomond.

WILL: Aren't they, Stephen, they're good lads?

(*They all look at STEPHEN.*)

STEPHEN: Yeah.

WILL: Ay.

(*He continues singing.*)

By Yon Bonnie Banks

MIKE: This place is far out, man. And when I say far out I don't mean it in the hippie sense. I mean far out in the middle of nowhere. We put up the tent last night in this field. But I slept in the car. I wasn't going to put up with that lot snoring and farting all night. When I woke up all

I could see through the windscreen was mountains, man.
Fucking mountains. And everything all red.
(*STEPHEN enters and takes a photo.*
MIKE jumps.)
What you doing?

STEPHEN: Nothing

MIKE: Creeping round like that!
(*They look at the mountains.*
DARREN can be seen giving WILL his morphine.)

MIKE: The sun's rising.

STEPHEN: Mmm.

MIKE: Look at that mountain. There's clouds on the top
of it.

STEPHEN: It's great.

MIKE: It's shit.
(*They look.*)
I mean you don't expect the land to go up in the clouds,
do ya?

STEPHEN: I s'pose not.

MIKE: Well, it does here.

STEPHEN: Yeah.

MIKE: It's crap. Here comes the sun. Come on ya wanker!
Look, it's like a great big football, innit?

STEPHEN: Mmm.

MIKE: Like some tosser in Australia booted it into the sky last
night and it's coming up over England this morning.

STEPHEN: Scotland.

MIKE: Whatever. Come on, get up there you lazy sod!

STEPHEN: It's rising.

MIKE: Come on! Come on! Yeessss! Wow! Some trip man.
I'm not even stoned.
(*He cheers.*
STEPHEN takes another photo.)
Take one of me!
(*MIKE poses for STEPHEN.*
They laugh.
DARREN enters.)

DARREN: What's going on?

MIKE: Ain't you got eyes?

DARREN: Oh yeah, sunrise.

MIKE: Alright, is he?

DARREN: (*Defensively.*) Yeah, course he is. Says we have to head for Fortwilliam.

STEPHEN: We have to get some petrol.

MIKE: No we don't. You can go for miles on reserve.

DARREN: What we having for breakfast?

MIKE: I don't know. (*To STEPHEN.*) What is there?

STEPHEN: Bread.

MIKE: Want more than bread, don't I?

STEPHEN: You ate all the smoked salmon.

(*He goes.*)

MIKE: (*Under his breath.*) Wanker.

DARREN: Yeah, wanker.

In the Blooming Heather

MIKE: So we headed up into them mountains. They only got two petrol stations in Scotland I reckon. They got one in Edinburgh and one in Glasgow.

DARREN: What we going to do?

MIKE: I don't know.

STEPHEN: There was that village place. That might have a garage.

WILL: It's a fair way back.

DARREN: Is that Ben Nevis, Grandad?

WILL: Ay, I reckon.

DARREN: And what's that one?

WILL: That could be Ben Nevis now you come to mention it.

STEPHEN: (*Pointing at a third mountain.*) Actually Will, from the map it looks like it's more likely to be that one.

WILL: Is that so?

STEPHEN: Think so.

WILL: Ah well you might be right at that.

DARREN: That one looks bigger.

MIKE: I can't believe you lot. Here we are stuck in the middle of nowhere and all you can talk about is which of them mountains is Ben Nevis.

WILL: Don't get yourself upset, Mike. We've got the tent.

MIKE: I'm not staying here all night. We've run out of fags.

WILL: (*Alarmed.*) Have we?

MIKE: All there is here is sheep. Look at that one standing in the middle of the road. (*Shouting at the sheep.*) Roads are for cars. Look at it! Couldn't be arsed. Standing there with that gormless expression. Looks like Darren! How far is it back to that village?

STEPHEN: Fifteen miles.

MIKE: Shit!

STEPHEN: You could take a shortcut up there.

MIKE: I'm not walking up a mountain.

STEPHEN: Be quicker.

MIKE: You coming, Darren?

DARREN: How long will it take?

STEPHEN: Few hours.
    (*DARREN looks at WILL.*)
    I'll look after him.

DARREN: No you won't. (*To MIKE.*) Better stay with me Grandad.

MIKE: Oh right.

DARREN: You going on your own?

MIKE: I don't know.

WILL: You go with him, Stephen.

STEPHEN: (*Looking at MIKE.*) Shall I?

MIKE: (*Leaving.*) Do what you like.

WILL: Go on, Stephen.

STEPHEN: See you.
    (*STEPHEN and MIKE go.*
    WILL winces with pain.)

DARREN: You alright?

WILL: Need a pish.
    (*They go.*)

Lost in Lochaber

MIKE enters, followed by STEPHEN.

STEPHEN: Wait a minute, can't you?

MIKE: You still looking at that map?

STEPHEN: I have to, don't I?

MIKE: I'm going this way.

STEPHEN: You'll get lost.

MIKE: Well, which way is it?

STEPHEN: I don't know.

MIKE: You're the one with the map.

STEPHEN: We can either carry on along this ridge or else climb up there.

MIKE: Well, this is the way we want to go ain't it?

STEPHEN: Yeah, but I think there might be like a gully in between here and where we want to get to. But if we go up there we can get round.

MIKE: Well, come on then.

STEPHEN: But…

MIKE: Come on. Stop farting around. Tosser.
(*He goes.*
STEPHEN follows.)
One minute I was walking in the sun and everything was sweet and the next minute this mist came down and you couldn't see three foot in front of you. Where did the pissing mist come from? That's what I want to know.

STEPHEN: It's the cloud.

MIKE: What is?

STEPHEN: The mist.

MIKE: What, the cloud decided to come down and sit on the mountain?

STEPHEN: Yes.

MIKE: Clouds are meant to be in the sky. Get off this mountain you lazy sod.

STEPHEN: I can't work out which way's North.

MIKE: You wanker. Hello! Hello!

STEPHEN: They won't hear us.

MIKE: Hello! Shit. This is really getting to me, man. I'm not used to being in the middle of nowhere.

STEPHEN: We'll just have to wait for it to lift.

MIKE: It's dark. Hello! Hello! Help!

(*He listens.*)

What was that?

STEPHEN: What?

(*They listen.*)

MIKE: That! Hello!

(*They listen.*)

STEPHEN: It's a sheep.

MIKE: No, it's not. It's them. Hello!

(*They listen.*)

STEPHEN: It's a sheep.

MIKE: Shit. Well, let's go that way.

STEPHEN: If we stay here and wait for it to lift I'll be able to get my bearings. If we move then we won't know where we are.

MIKE: I know exactly where we are. On this mountain in the middle of the pissing mist. Just my luck to be stuck here with you.

(*Pause.*)

When I was a kid I got lost at the fair up Hampstead. I was only four or something. When they found me my Dad got me by the arm and shook me so hard he dislocated it.

(*Pause.*)

I'm dying for a fag.

STEPHEN: Want a spliff?

MIKE: You what?

STEPHEN: Want some blow?

MIKE: You got some blow?

STEPHEN: Yeah.

MIKE: Well, why didn't you say so?

(*STEPHEN gets out a ready-made joint and some matches.*)

You been having weed on the sly?

STEPHEN: No.

MIKE: Where'd you get this?

STEPHEN: From Edward's garden.

MIKE: He your lecturer?

STEPHEN: Yes.

MIKE: Great what you can get away with if you live in a posh house. (*Smoking the joint.*) So you're on first name terms.

STEPHEN: Eh?

MIKE: With your lecturer.

STEPHEN: Oh yeah.

MIKE: Is he your boyfriend?

STEPHEN: Piss off.

MIKE: Just asking.

STEPHEN: Well, he's not. He lives with this other bloke.

MIKE: Your Dad know?

STEPHEN: What?

MIKE: You living with two gays.

STEPHEN: No.

MIKE: He was some sort of reverend at the Pentecostal Church wasn't he, your Dad?

STEPHEN: Yeah.

MIKE: So why ain't you living at home? Get chucked out?

STEPHEN: No.

MIKE: I got chucked out.

STEPHEN: I left.

MIKE: Why?

STEPHEN: Just did.

(*They smoke.*)

MIKE: So why did you try to top yourself?

STEPHEN: I didn't.

MIKE: It's what I heard.

STEPHEN: You keeping that?

MIKE: (*Handing STEPHEN the joint.*) I heard you was in a loony bin.

STEPHEN: Well I wasn't.

MIKE: Alright.

STEPHEN: I just had to go and see this woman. A counsellor.

MIKE: Why?

STEPHEN: I got depressed.

(*Pause.*)

MIKE: So what did you have to do?

STEPHEN: When?

MIKE: When you went to see your counsellor.

STEPHEN: Load of stuff.

MIKE: Like what?

STEPHEN: You don't want to know.

MIKE: I do.

STEPHEN: I had to like pretend my Dad, or my Mum or someone was a cushion and then talk to them.

MIKE: You didn't.

STEPHEN: Yeah. You had to tell people what you felt about them and then forgive them.

MIKE: What like, you had a cushion in front of you and you talked to it?

STEPHEN: Yeah.

MIKE: 'Kin 'ell.

STEPHEN: There was this red one that was my Dad. And a blue one that was my Mum. Sometimes there was so many of them I forgot who was who.

MIKE: And this was supposed to stop you going mad?

STEPHEN: That's right.

(*They start laughing uncontrollably.*)

Yours was brown.

MIKE: You what?

STEPHEN: There was one cushion that was you.

MIKE: You're kidding.

STEPHEN: No. And I had to say things like 'I forgive you for pissing in my trainers, Mike'.

MIKE: I never did.

STEPHEN: In the changing rooms after football.

MIKE: Don't remember that.

(*They smoke.*)

And what was it meant to do?

STEPHEN: Stop you carrying all that stuff around with you.

(*Pause.*)

You know at school.

MIKE: Yeah.

STEPHEN: Know what I used to call you?

MIKE: What?

STEPHEN: Freddy Krueger.
  (*STEPHEN laughs.*
  MIKE doesn't.)
STEPHEN: Remember *Nightmare on Elm Street*?
MIKE: Yeah.
  (*STEPHEN laughs more.*)
STEPHEN: I chose a brown cushion for you because of the
  dog turd you put in my locker.
  (*He finds this even funnier.*)
MIKE: It all sounds like a load of bollocks.
STEPHEN: Mmm.
MIKE: Load of crap.
STEPHEN: How do you know?
MIKE: Didn't do you any good, did it??
STEPHEN: Might have.
MIKE: Crap.
STEPHEN: You should try it.
MIKE: Why?
STEPHEN: 'Cos you probably need to.
MIKE: What you mean?
STEPHEN: Well, your Dad bullied you, didn't he?
MIKE: No.
STEPHEN: You said he dislocated your arm.
MIKE: That was years ago.
STEPHEN: And then you ended up being a bully at school.
MIKE: No I never.
STEPHEN: Look pretend that rock – right? – is your Dad.
MIKE: Piss off.
STEPHEN: Go on, say what you want to say to him. Say, 'I
  hate you, you bastard'.
MIKE: No. I'm not a headcase like you, mate. Don't need
  crap like that.
STEPHEN: You're scared.
MIKE: You got an arsehole for a mouth.
STEPHEN: Coward.
MIKE: Piss off!
STEPHEN: Say it then. Say, 'Dad, you're a bastard but I
  forgive you'.

MIKE: No.

STEPHEN: You want to end up like him?

MIKE: What?

STEPHEN: Say it.

MIKE: I'm warning you!

STEPHEN: Actually you're like him already.

(*MIKE headbutts STEPHEN.*)

MIKE: I warned you. I fucking warned you. But you wouldn't
listen. Would ya? I told you not to push it. That was your
trouble. You was always pushing it, Hurdy. Nobody tells
me who I gotta forgive. If I forgive him then it means it
don't matter. And it does. It matters. I hate the fucker. I'm
never forgiving him.

(*Long pause.*

STEPHEN is holding his nose.)

I'm freezing.

(*Pause.*)

What time is it?

(*STEPHEN doesn't answer.*)

Eh?

STEPHEN: Half twelve.

MIKE: Come over here.

STEPHEN: What?

MIKE: We gotta keep warm.

(*STEPHEN looks at him.*)

Come on! Wanna die of exposure, do you?

(*STEPHEN still doesn't move.*)

You'd rather die?

(*They shiver.*)

You wanker!

(*He goes to STEPHEN.*

*They awkwardly huddle together trying to find the best way of
keeping warm.*)

Keep still.

Keep still I said.

What's wrong with you?

Tosser!

(*He elbows STEPHEN.*
STEPHEN flips.)

STEPHEN: Don't you hit me. Don't you ever fucking hit me again.

(*He grabs MIKE by the throat and pins him down.*
There is a violent struggle.)

MIKE: Get off! Get off me.

(*They look each other in the eyes.*
STEPHEN climbs off MIKE and moves away.)

Shit!

(*They sit and shiver.*)

Look.

STEPHEN: What?

MIKE: We gotta keep warm.

(*STEPHEN looks at him for a moment.*
They edge towards each other. They huddle together trying to find the best way to keep warm.
STEPHEN is shivering with cold and fear.)

Grandad and Grandson

WILL: It was just a wee village with one pub and a kirk.

DARREN: Yeah?

WILL: And everybody knew everybody else and looked out for each other.

(*He winces in pain.*)

DARREN: You alright?

WILL: There's no even a wee drop of the diamorphin left?

DARREN: No.

WILL: Never mind, lad, never mind.

DARREN: Those wankers.

WILL: It's okay, laddie. Of course it had its drawbacks. Everybody knew your business as well. I had a fight with Kenneth Anderson on my way home from school one day and my mother knew about it by the time I was home. That's why I left, you see. I wanted my freedom. I wanted a good job and money and a car. So I went to England. But now…

DARREN: What?

WILL: Folk don't look after each other any more. They just get on with their lives. They see a body lying in the road and they walk on by. No Good Samaritans these days. (*He winces.*)

You make sure you keep out of trouble. Okay? That Mike, he's a good lad, isn't he?

DARREN: Yeah!

WILL: He'll look after you. Eh?

DARREN: Yes.

WILL: I did my best for you but I should have done more. I'm sorry, lad.

DARREN: Shut up, Grandad! Shut up! Those wankers, where are they? Leaving us here like this! Wankers!

WILL: Shhh! (*Singing to comfort DARREN.*)

'Speed bonnie boat like a bird on a wing

On with the sailors' cry.

Carry the lad that was born to be king

Over the sea to Skye.'

(*He fades and DARREN holds him.*

MIKE and STEPHEN appear at the entrance to the tent.)

DARREN: Where you been, man?

MIKE: Where do you think we've been? At a rave with some sheep. We got lost.

DARREN: We ran out of diamorphin.

STEPHEN: Maybe we should get him to hospital.

DARREN: He doesn't want to go to hospital.

MIKE: (*Placatory.*) Alright, Darren.

DARREN: What does he know about anything?

MIKE: He's only trying to help.

DARREN: Fat lot of help he is. He got you lost.

MIKE: Weren't his fault.

DARREN: Tosser.

WILL: (*Faintly.*) Darren.

(*DARREN goes to him.*)

Take me home.

DARREN: To London?

WILL: To Skye.

MIKE: Come on. Let's get him in the car. Here, Stephen, bring it over, will ya?

(*He hands STEPHEN the keys.*)

STEPHEN: Okay.

(*They smile at each other in acknowledgement of the irony. DARREN looks at MIKE in disgust.*)

Over the sea to Skye.

MIKE: It was a stroke what got Darren's Grandad in the end. Not the cancer. Funny word – stroke. Like God's leaned out of heaven and run his hand over ya. He got a thrombosis. His veins were so messed up from all the smoking so his blood clotted. That's a what a thrombosis is. It stopped the flow of blood to his brain. We didn't get him all the way to Skye. But we could see it in the distance. We stopped and wheeled him to the top of this hill and you could see it in the distance. 'Least we did that for him.

STEPHEN: Yeah.

(*DARREN is with WILL who is now dead.*
MIKE and STEPHEN are at a distance watching.)

MIKE: I never seen a dead person before.

STEPHEN: I saw my Gran.

MIKE: Remember going to Madame Tussaud's with the school?

STEPHEN: Yeah.

MIKE: That's what he looks like. One of them wax models.

STEPHEN: Yeah.

MIKE: Makes you think.

STEPHEN: What?

MIKE: I dunno. 'Bout what you do with your life I s'pose.

The Grave

MIKE: So there we was. On Skye. In a churchyard. Couldn't afford the funeral so Darren got hold of Skid on his mobile and he turned up in this flash car his mate had leant him. Had lots of dosh to chuck around. Paid the undertaker, everything.

(*DARREN sprinkles earth into the hole.*)

SKID: So who wants a lift back to Glasgow?

MIKE: Gotta get the car back to London.

SKID: You what?

MIKE: What?

SKID: (*Indicating STEPHEN.*) He can do that? Tell you mate, London's tame in comparison to what's going down up here. Kid's play. See that car? My mate's got three of them. Says I can borrow it whenever I like.

MIKE: Right.

SKID: I mean what's there for you in London? Let's see assault, TWOC, criminal damage, dangerous driving. What you think you'll get for that? I'd say anything from six months to a year in the nick.

STEPHEN: He might get probation.

SKID: What's he doing here? This your social worker, Mike?

MIKE: Piss off.

SKID: Did you ask him here, Darren?

DARREN: No.

(*MIKE looks at DARREN.*)

SKID: I got a present for you, Darren.

DARREN: What?

SKID: Something to cheer you up a bit. But you'll have to come to the car with me to take it.

DARREN: What is it?

SKID: Duhhh! Well it's white and powdery.

MIKE: He don't need that now, Skid.

SKID: What's with you?

MIKE: I just think it's not what he needs today.

SKID: Let him be the judge of that.

MIKE: Alright.

SKID: Gone straight, have you Mike? Your little friend here turned you soft?

MIKE: Piss off.

SKID: You running out on us, Mike?

MIKE: Don't talk crap.

SKID: You know I don't like people running out on me. Nobody runs out on me.

MIKE: I'm not running out on you.

SKID: I always did have you down to be Ray Liotta, Mikey. The grass.

MIKE: And who are you? Joe Pesci? The psycho?

SKID: That's right.

(*SKID quotes Tommy's lines in* Goodfellas *to STEPHEN, from 'Hey Spider, that fucking bandage…'.*
STEPHEN replies with Spider's line.
SKID is taken aback that STEPHEN knows the scene.
MIKE laughs. He quotes Jimmy's lines, from 'Attaboy, Spider.'
He laughs again.
SKID looks at him. Suddenly he reaches into his jacket and pulls out a gun. He points it at STEPHEN's head.
Everyone freezes.)

SKID: Oooh that's wiped the smiles off your faces, innit?

MIKE: Skid.

SKID: Look at him Mike, he's nobody. He's nothing. He don't count.

MIKE: Leave him, Skid.

SKID: I could do it. Who do you wanna be, Mike? The bloke holding the gun or the one who sucks on it?

MIKE: Come on, Skid.

SKID: Your choice. You wanna end up coughing your lungs up in some squalid council flat? That what you want?

MIKE: Don't be stupid.

SKID: You haven't answered me. Which would you rather be? Say I'd rather be the one sucking on the gun and I'll let him go.

MIKE: Look, Skid –

SKID: All you gotta do is answer.

(*STEPHEN whimpers.*)

MIKE: It's alright. He won't do it.

SKID: (*Priming the gun.*) Want a bet?

MIKE: (*Really scared.*) Skid!

SKID: Just say it. Go on, 'I'd rather…'

MIKE: I'd rather not end up on a murder charge.

SKID: (*Forcing the gun into STEPHEN's mouth.*) Say it.

MIKE: What?

SKID: I'd rather be the sucker.

MIKE: I'd rather be the sucker.

SKID: (*Releasing STEPHEN.*) That's what I thought. You coming, Darren?

DARREN: You got anything apart from wiz, Skid?

SKID: I'll see what I can do.

MIKE: Darren.

SKID: Bye kids.

> (*DARREN and SKID go.*
> *STEPHEN retches.*)

MIKE: It's alright. He's a psycho but he wouldn't have done it.

STEPHEN: Bastard.

MIKE: I thought you were supposed to forgive and forget.

STEPHEN: Fucking bastard!

MIKE: See?

STEPHEN: What?

MIKE: There's some things that can't be forgiven.

> (*A baby cries.*)

A Year Later

MIKE: I got hundred and eighty hours community service. They took it into account that I was starting college. (*To the baby.*) Shut up! I'm a sort of house husband now, whatever they call it. I have to look after him when me girlfriend's out at work. Steve comes round sometimes and takes pictures of us. He's doing a project on fathers and sons. (*Baby cries.*)
Why don't you stop that?
(*Baby cries.*)
Haven't seen much of the old crowd. Saw Darren a couple of months ago outside Woolworths with his dog. They were both looking pretty scummy.

A Homeless Boy and His Dog

DARREN: Spare some change, mate?

MIKE: Darren!

DARREN: Oh, hi man.

MIKE: It's Mike, Darren.

DARREN: Oh, Mike, yeah, right.

MIKE: How are you?

DARREN: I'm alright. You got anything on you, Mike?

MIKE: What you mean, Darren?

DARREN: You always used to have some pills or some wiz.

MIKE: I'm clean nowadays man.

DARREN: Right. You know it's been hard what with me
Grandad dying. I'm still sort of in mourning like man.

MIKE: Right.

DARREN: So if you had any money you could lend us, man.
It's been hard you know man. Got thrown out the flat.

MIKE: Maybe I should have said he could come round here
stay for a while. But the baby was just born and... I'm
sorry mate. You tried Skid?

DARREN: Haven't seen him lately. He's a bit pissed off
with me.

MIKE: How come?

DARREN: Thinks I've been tiefing off him. I ain't.

MIKE: Right. Well why don't you come to the council with
me? We could try and sort something out.

DARREN: Yeah good idea.

MIKE: We could go now.

DARREN: I can't now man. I got this spot for another hour.

MIKE: Well look, here's my phone number. I'll ask around
for you.

DARREN: Thanks man. You got any money? Just to tide
me over.

MIKE: Here.

DARREN: Oh right.

MIKE: I'll see you then.

DARREN: Yeah. See ya. (*To passers by.*) Spare some change?

MIKE: Bye, Darren. You'll ring me. Yeah?

DARREN: Spare some change?

MIKE: He never did phone me. Haven't seen him since.
Seen Skid though. Hanging out with the kids on the estate,

dealing. Cruising round in his car. Flash. Very flash. Aston Martin.

Home Sweet Home

Noise of a baby crying.

MIKE: (*Picking the baby up.*) Stop it.
   (*He paces with the baby.*)
   I got responsibilities now. Gotta think of the future. You need determination and a bit of good luck to stop you like going off the rails. And you gotta keep out of harm's way.
   (*He looks out the window again.*
   SKID is outside dealing. He looks up at MIKE's window.)
   So I keep myself to myself. Stay in and watching the telly. It's better than being on the streets. Safer. Wiser.
   (*MIKE and SKID look at each other.*
   STEPHEN takes photos of him.
   MIKE paces with baby. Suddenly he stops and looks out.)
   Just stop it.

The End.

OTHER PLAYS FOR YOUNG PEOPLE BY PHILIP OSMENT

Duck!
9781840028225

Little Violet and the Angel
9781840022179

The Palace of Fear
9781840025057

COLLECTIONS FOR YOUNG PEOPLE

Class Acts: New Plays for Children to Act
The Acme Thunderer, The Wish Collector
& Of The Terrifying Events of the Hamlin Estate
By Lin Coghlan, Oladipo Agboluaje & Philip Osment
9781840029338

PLAYS FOR ADULTS BY PHILIP OSMENT

Inside
9781849430234

Buried Alive
9781840021974

The Undertaking
9781870259873

WWW.OBERONBOOKS.COM

Follow us on www.twitter.com/@oberonbooks
& www.facebook.com/oberonbook

9 781840 022728